MANUAL

basic studio directing

media

MANUAL

media

MANUAL

basic studio
directing

rod fairweather

Focal Press

OXFORD   BOSTON   JOHANNESBURG   MELBOURNE   NEW DELHI   SINGAPORE

Focal Press
An imprint of Butterworth-Heinemann
Linacre House, Jordan Hill, Oxford OX2 8DP
225 Wildwood Avenue, Woburn MA 01801-2041
A division of Reed Educational and Professional Publishing Ltd

A member of the Reed Elsevier plc group

First published 1998
Transferred to digital printing 2001

© Reed Educational and Professional Publishing Ltd 1998

British Library Cataloguing in Publication Data
A catalogue record for this book is available from the British Library

Library of Congress Cataloguing in Publication Data
A catalogue record for this book is available from the Library of Congress

ISBN 0 240 51525 0

For information on all Focal Press publications
visit our website at www.focalpress.com

FOR EVERY TITLE THAT WE PUBLISH, BUTTERWORTH-HEINEMANN
WILL PAY FOR BTCV TO PLANT AND CARE FOR A TREE.

Contents

Introduction

Television studios shoot a great range of programmes – dramas, music, news, children's programmes, comedies etc. Each genre uses specialised skills, but they share a core of basic directing techniques and language.

This book focuses on the directing skills common to all programmes. I will spend very little time talking about the script and front of camera performance – this is where the genres split into their own worlds.

Whatever you're directing you'll need to provide the crew with the right information at the right time, and understand enough of their roles to be able to explain what you want, and help them through difficulties they may be facing.

I refer to live television on a number of occasions. At one time it was assumed that single camera shooting and post production would take over from multi-camera studios, but live television turns out to be surprisingly cost effective.

One significant group – news and current affairs – continues to do live programming for editorial reasons. You cannot do an up-to-the-moment news programme if you are not live. There is a lot of N&CA directing across the world which uses the basic techniques in this book, but uses them at high speed and in a technically complex environment.

It is difficult to get the opportunity to practise directing. Nobody wants directors learning on air, so it's vital that you have a realistic chance of pulling off a clean (mistake-free) programme before you sit down. The better prepared you are for your early programmes the better you will perform, and the more likely you are to be invited back.

Finally, I firmly believe that television directing is not brain surgery. You don't need a stream of degrees to be a good director. You do need to enjoy it.

Acknowledgements

My thanks to my wife Lana, who has put as much time and effort, and a great deal more patience into this book than I have.

Thanks also to everyone who went out of their way to provide photographs. They are reprinted courtesy of 124 Facilities, Anglia Television, Autocue, Bazal Productions, BBC News 24, BBC TV, B Sky B, GMTV Magazine, ITN, NBC, New Delhi Television, Optex, Sony Broadcast, Tektronics and TWI. *Food and Drink* script reproduced by courtesy of the BBC. *Food and Drink* is produced by Bazal for the BBC.

Note: Throughout this book I refer to 'his' on a number of occasions. Please take it as read that all information is aimed equally at both the sexes, and it is simply to stop the text becoming too tedious by constantly saying 'his or her'. There is nothing in studio directing that makes it more suitable as a career for one gender over the other.

Directing skills

Programmes need good directors. Not just the shows that turn out looking great, but the ones that totter on the edge of disaster.

Let's look at a live news programme where you have plenty of time to plan, rehearse and refine. By the time transmission comes along everyone knows exactly what is needed of them. They know all their sources and cues, so when you're on air there really is very little for you to say. The programme flows smoothly, confidently and comes off air on time.

The other scenario is when there is little or no rehearsal time. The running order changes rapidly and the technology falls to pieces around your ears (which actually happens more often than most people realise). If a major news story breaks producers will be trying to set up live injects, tapes will be edited very late, or go out of date so fast they need to be re-edited. New information comes continuously to the programme editor and presenters.

In this situation if you manage to get a clean programme out, with the presenters always knowing what they are doing next, into which camera, linking accurately into the right videotape or live inject, then the viewers at home will have no idea of the controlled chaos going on behind the scenes.

Clarity of vision

The key to holding this type of show together is for the director to know exactly what is happening next, and what options are available. You may not know what the programme editor wants until 10 seconds before the end of a VT, but if you know the state of everything around you 10 seconds will be enough. However, in the previous minute you should be thoroughly across everything going on. What VTs are instantly available to you? If there is a live link coming in, is it usable? Have all the communications been checked through sound? Does the person at the other end know what's going to happen? Does the presenter have the latest information?

When the editor does make their decision you should know instantly if it will work. You should also have another plan up your sleeve in case it won't (bear in mind that the editor will be up to their eyeballs at the time and may not be aware the inject cannot hear the programme sound, so can't be used).

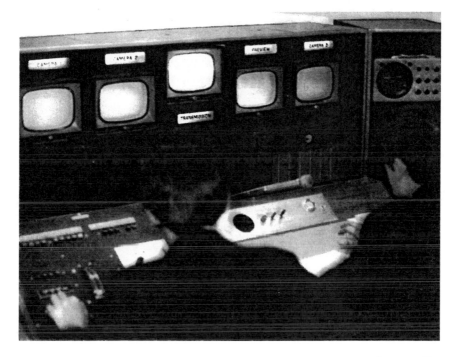

Control rooms have grown more complex in the last forty years. Non-technical changes include fashions – some control rooms haven't seen suits in decades.

Communication skills

It is up to you to let the right people know the information they need to do the job properly. There is no point in saying 'Cut and cue' if the sound supervisor doesn't know what you are cutting to.

All instructions must be clear, precise and brief

Lead when a lead is needed

Get everyone working in the same direction at the same time. The worst directing in a crisis is when the director says nothing. Vision mixers guess one thing is next, camera operators guess another while sound guess a completely different option.

Say what you want

Teamwork

When the pressure is on, you must work with your team. Let them get on with their jobs, and you get on with yours.

Do not concentrate on one particular area. There is a tendency, particularly if you have come through one of the technical operations, to spend too much time making sure the person doing your old job is doing it properly.

Let your team do the work for you

Shouting

There was a time when ranting and raving in a control room was seen as the sign of a strong director. Most people now realise it usually means the director has lost the plot. Shouting gets in the way of useful talkback, and throws additional pressure on operators who are probably already under undue stress.

Do not shout unless there is a dangerous situation and you need 100 per cent attention from everyone immediately

Aptitude

Without question some people are more suited to studio directing than others. However, it often takes many months for the best directors to shine in the job. There is a tendency to believe that only those who pick up the job quickly will be any good. This is not the case. One trainee director may have spent far longer in studios than others, so you should expect them to progress quicker in the early stages.

Don't expect to be brilliant from day one

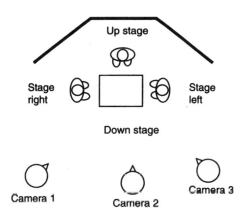

Basic stage areas

Central to effective communication is using the same language and references as everyone else.

If you are directing and need a prop or performer to move, use the stage terms to clarify where you want them to go.

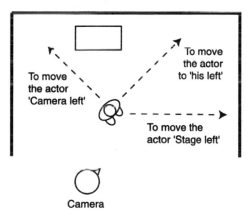

Three different references for left and right

The hardest descriptions to explain clearly are 'left' and 'right'. You will normally see the action through a monitor in the production control room, showing the view from a camera. To move anything, be clear if you are referring to 'Camera left', 'his left' or 'Stage left'.

13

Working with the production team

The producer is responsible for the programme content. If it is a long programme or a programme that's on air every day there will be a programme
editor who has a number of producers working under him.

The role of the director is to make the script work on screen. While producers, researchers etc. work to the editor, all the studio technical staff
work to the director.

Who's the boss?

This question regularly crops up and is completely irrelevant. The producer
and the director must work as a team. I don't expect a director to override
the content the producer wants unless it is absolutely necessary, which
usually means it is not technically possible.

The technical crews must all follow the director. If a producer starts
yelling instructions over the director's shoulder there is a danger that half
the crew will do what the producer says, the other half what the director
says. Needless to say this is the surest route to disaster.

A director must always have something ready to put on air, so if you have
not been told what is next have something up your sleeve. You cannot cut
back to your presenter with nothing to do.

If anything goes horribly wrong I expect the director to make the immediate decisions. You will be in a far better position to make whatever call is
necessary as you should be aware of what options are open to you.

Managing the team

Most crews work very hard to give the director a first-class product. People
who have made a special effort are far more likely to repeat it if you
acknowledge their efforts and thank them. It's not hard, but a skill many
directors have not spent long enough developing.

Making mistakes

If you make a mistake, say so. Nobody respects a director who refuses to
admit when they were wrong. The worst mistake you can make is to blame
other people for your errors. Trust me, everyone knows when the director
is at fault. So impress everyone and admit to it.

The programme director working with the programme editor before the live transmission. Being aware of the editor's intentions early gives time for potential problems to be cleared up before everyone moves into the studio.

Even though this programme is being prepared on an electronic newsroom system which can be viewed anywhere in the building, it is still helpful for the director to be based near the rest of the production team.

Presentation

It is easy to think of your programme in isolation, and to forget that we are all just a small part of the bigger picture – the network.

In the centre of any network is the presentation department, sometimes known as Transmission. They physically transmit programmes, trails, adverts etc. from a network control room that looks similar to a small studio control room, except that instead of having cameras on preview monitors there are studios.

Computers often control much of the transmission, but there still needs to be a network director (or transmission controller) to make decisions and to check details.

How networks function

Most television channels have a system of a central transmission point or network centre. Their signal (or 'feed') is sent out to other parts of the country where there are local studio and transmission facilities. For large chunks of the day the output will be the network centre feed, but these regional transmission sites can switch to local studios to broadcast their own programmes or 'opt-outs'.

Regional opt-outs

Typically these are local news summaries, evening news programmes and local sports shows.

For regional opt-outs to work smoothly the regional centre must be able to make a clean switch away from, and back to, the network transmission. This means every regional centre producing programmes of exactly the same fixed length, starting and finishing to within a split second.

The central network offers suitable points during the day for regional transmission suites to switch to local studios. At the end of the agreed duration, the network director counts the regions back into the main network. The switch can either be done manually at the regional centre, or controlled by the network centre, sending out control pulses hidden at the top of the screen.

Note that even if every regional centre in a country is switching away from the network centre, there must still be a usable picture on the network feed. Very occasionally there will be a problem with one of the switches. If a region fails to switch away you don't want any old rubbish accidentally going to air.

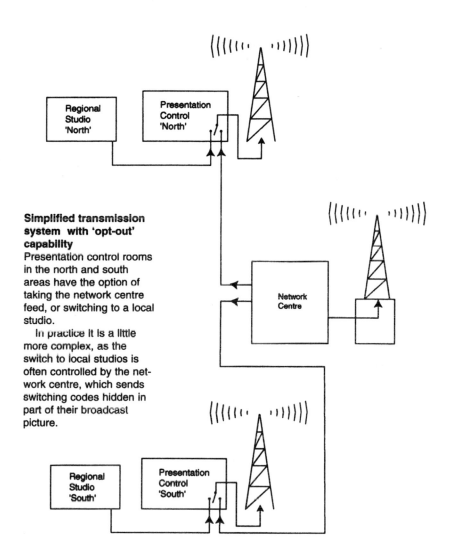

Simplified transmission system with 'opt-out' capability

Presentation control rooms in the north and south areas have the option of taking the network centre feed, or switching to a local studio.

In practice it is a little more complex, as the switch to local studios is often controlled by the network centre, which sends switching codes hidden in part of their broadcast picture.

17

Network directors

The main aim of a network director (or transmission controller) is to run a smooth, clean transmission, with programmes starting on time, promotions running at appropriate points and all commercial requirements fulfilled.

Timing of a network

Most networks have fixed points – usually for the main evening news programmes – which often start at precisely the top of the hour. To achieve this level of accuracy takes a great deal of work and skill, and the presentation department is dependent on information from programme makers to be precise. It is inexcusable for quoted programme durations to be inaccurate – it will invariably result in the network looking messy and amateurish.

Programme identification

More than anything, network directors want to know they are putting the right programme to air. Clear, accurate clocks are vital for pre-recorded programmes. If a studio is going live to air then the studio engineer will line up with presentation, ensuring picture and sound are getting through, and confirm programme details.

Commercial considerations

Failing to play out adverts on a commercial channel is financial suicide. If they don't go out, the money doesn't come in, so you can't make any more programmes. Frustrating though it may sometimes be, commercials will usually take priority over everything bar national disasters.

Live programmes

If a programme is live, the production assistant will liaise with the network director confirming on-air time and exact duration. A network director will usually want to know how the programme is to start (so that they know what transition to use joining your titles), how it will end, the names of the presenters (for continuity announcements) and any special instructions.

If you plan deliberately to imitate tape spooling, or fade to black or silence during either a live or pre-recorded programme you must clearly inform the network director, who might otherwise mistake it for a breakdown. You have no idea how embarrassing it is to apologise for a mistake, only to find there wasn't a mistake to apologise for.

Terrestial

Broadcast from aerials on the ground.
You need many aerials to cover a large
country, but have the option of regional
variations in the transmitted signal (i.e.
the transmitter switches to a local studio
for some part of the day).

Direct to home, satellite

Broadcast via an uplink to a geostationary
satellite, which retransmits it to small
satellite receivers at the viewers' homes.
Satellites are expensive and have a limited
lifespan, but cover difficult terrain (e.g.
mountains) without any problems

Cable

A cable company picks up one or more
satellite signals, and redistributes
them by cable or fibre optic to local
houses. Viewers can see pictures
from many different satellites but
cables have to be laid by the company
to distribute the signals. Houses look
tidier without aerials or satellite dishes.

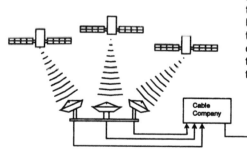

Transmission Systems

Studio cameras

As a relatively new director it is unlikely you will have a choice of, or even be interested in, the cameras used on the floor. The important point is that they should match each other, so that there is no visual jump in colour, resolution or picture quality when you cut between them.

CCD/tubes
The bit of the camera that detects light used to be a camera tube. Since the late 1980s tubes have been superseded by CCDs (charge-coupled devices), which is a type of electronic chip that responds to light.

CCDs have a number of advantages. They are much easier to line up, are more stable, handle overly bright lights better, are cheaper and lighter.

Frankly, using tube cameras was a bit of a pain.

Lightweight/heavyweight
One of the decisions you may have to make is how many cameras to use, and what type. You may not have much choice – hiring in additional cameras is expensive and time-consuming.

There is now precious little difference between large studio cameras and lightweight cameras. The choice of lens has far more impact, as the electronics in both types are virtually identical.

Studio cameras have good, large viewfinders, and the camera controls are usually more comfortably configured than lightweight cameras.

The big difference is usually the lens, although lightweight cameras can have large lenses attached to them.

The lens is a large part of the weight and cost of a studio camera. Do not risk damaging / dropping it. You will be fired.

Using lightweight cameras in a studio
Generally you will be better off using the main studio cameras. However, you may need to get a camera into a small space, in which case it makes sense to use a lightweight camera.

Clearly if you want hand-held shots as part of the programme style, then you need lightweight cameras. Operators aren't as hardy as they used to be.

Lightweight and full studio cameras can be matched to give directors great flexibility. Talkback, exposure controls and reverse vision can all be sent down one cable. It is useful to have someone 'cable bashing' behind a handheld camera, making sure there is nothing to snag the cable.

21

Mounts and cranes

Standard studio pedestals (peds) are big, heavy and expensive. However, they let the camera operator pan, tilt, crab, track and elevate beautifully. They glide perfectly across a flat floor, but have a large footprint (i.e. they take up considerable floor space). If you have a small camera you want to squeeze into a tight space, then a lightweight tripod will be more useful.

Be aware of the limitations of standard peds. Typically they can elevate to 150 cm, or depress down to 65 cm. You may need to get lower, in which case you either need a different ped, or an arm mounted on top that allows the camera to get lower. (This may sound a contradiction in terms, but devices like the Dolphin Arm, allow a camera to be lowered to within a few inches of the floor).

Cranes
Do not climb onto a crane unless you have had crane safety training.

These used to be enormous heavy contraptions that physically lifted the camera operator with the camera. They required at least one other person driving, swinging or pushing it around. Large cranes needed a crew of five (one camera operator, two swingers, one driver and one person to clear a path in front of it).

Remote heads
Modern cranes tend to be operated from the ground by remote control. They are far smaller than the traditional designs, easier to transport, cheaper and can be operated with a smaller team. Typical is the Jimmy Jib, which can be up to 36 feet long, and operated by a single person.

For more exotic shots, advanced cranes like the Technocrane are available. This can produce a stunning range of shots, although it needs three people to operate it safely, and considerable expertise is needed to achieve some of the trickier movements.

The camera mount (the head) usually offers remote tilt, pan, zoom and focus. In addition some offer an additional axis of control, roll. This lets the camera rotate around the z-axis, useful when a camera can be tilted by more than ±90° (i.e. the shot goes upside down).

Do not expect a range of peds and cranes to be available at a moment's notice. If you know you are going to need a special mount, book it in advance and make sure you have the budget to pay for it. The camera crew should take care of safety and rigging of camera mounts. If you are planning on using an unusual crane make sure the senior camera operator is aware and familiar with it.

Courtesy New Delhi Television

A short Jimmy Jib gives opening and closing shots for this studio, and is able to reach comfortably into the lighting rig.

Lenses and f-numbers

There are a few technical terms about lenses you must understand as they affect the camera's pictures.

Focal length

If parallel light is shone into a lens the distance to the point of focus behind a lens is its focal length.

Image size

This is the size of the image as projected onto the pick-up device (i.e. the camera tube or CCD). Most broadcast cameras use 2/3 inch, although there are some other sizes in use, particularly in miniature and high definition cameras.

Angle of view

We can use the focal length (f), and the image size (y′) to calculate the horizontal angle of view (w):

$$w = 2 \tan^{-1} y'/ 2f$$

The good news is that I've never yet had to do this calculation. What is much more useful is looking up a manufacturer's specification to see what angle of view a lens covers. Most camera departments should have this information, or there are a number of manufacturers' sites on the Internet which give lens details.

f-numbers

We use an iris (a variable-sized hole) in a lens to control the amount of light let through. Obviously if a scene is dark we need to let more light through, so we open up the iris.

The f-number is our way of seeing how much light is let through the iris into the lens. The more we open the iris, the smaller the f-number. An f-number scale written on a lens looks like this:

  1.4   2   2.8   4   5.6   8   11   16   22

Each division, or 'stop', allows twice as much light through as the previous division.

Depth of field

Depth of field is the distance in front and behind your point of focus in which objects are still sharply in focus, and the trade-off in opening up an iris (letting more light through) is that the depth of field decreases. This may be an effect you want to use, i.e. isolating your subject from a busy background.

24

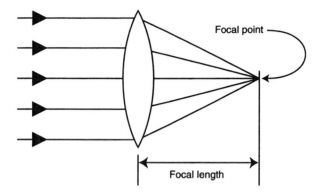

The focal length of a simple lens

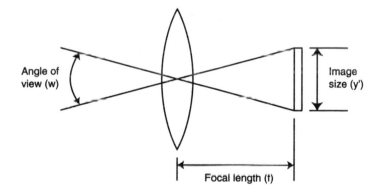

Angle of view of a fixed focal length lens

If you are using the formula for calculating the angle of view, make sure your measurements are all in the same units (i.e. a 2/3 inch CCD has a width of 8.6 mm).

Studio lenses

Prime lenses (fixed focal length) are rare in television (apart from special situations, e.g. hidden cameras), although they are still common in film.

Typical zoom lenses
Lightweight studio cameras with 2/3 inch CCDs will typically be fitted with something like a 14 × 8.5 f1.7 zoom lens, with a minimum focus distance of 0.8m. Large studio cameras will typically have a 55 × 9 zoom lens.

What this means is: the lightweight camera has a 14:1 zoom ratio. Its widest angle is 8.5 mm, equivalent to 54.4° horizontal angle of view, and tightest shot (14 × 8.5 mm) is 119 mm, or 4.14° horizontal angle of view. The widest the aperture can open to is f1.7 (on the wide end of its range).

If a 2× extender is built into the lens, it can effectively be changed to a 17–238 mm zoom lens, but it will have a reduced maximum aperture.

Note that lenses with the same focal lengths have different angles of view depending on the size of the pick-up (tube or CCD – typically 2/3 inch for studio cameras).

Wide angle
The main alternative lens you will come across is a wide angle lens for lightweight cameras. They are used when working in small sets (you may want to make the set look bigger than it really is), or when you have a lot of hand-held shots. A typical wide angle lens would be 9 × 5.2 f1.8, which can show a horizontal view of 80.5° down to 10.7°.

Practical application
If you have an accurate scaled floor plan, then you can work out if your cameras are able to give you the shot you want by drawing lines from your camera positions to the size of shot you require and measuring the angle.

Focusing and back focus
The correct way to focus is to zoom in as far as possible on the object you want, focus (on the eyes if shooting a person), then pull out to the shot size required. If the lens has been properly set up then the object will stay perfectly in focus no matter how much the operator zooms in and out. It also means if you suddenly decide you need the shot to zoom in, it will remain sharp all the way to the end stop.

If the focus does not stay sharp at the same distance for the entire zoom range, then the back focus (or flange back) needs adjusting. This is done either by experienced camera operators or engineers, and takes just a couple of minutes.

Lightweight camera with standard lens fitted with prompting unit and mounted on fully robotic pedestal. The operator in the control room can remotely move four cameras around the studio floor as well as controlling tilt, pan, zoom, focus and elevation.

The studio viewfinder and handle-mounted zoom and focus controls allow the camera to be used by a camera operator if necessary.

Standard shots (1)

There are a number of standard shot descriptions that are recognised around most of the world. All professional camera operators will be familiar with these terms, and should all offer the same shot sizes when asked. If you come up with your own terms for shots or, worse, use the standard shorthand words but do not mean what everyone else understands by them, you will slow down the production and look like an amateur.

The following descriptions apply to the 4 × 3 ratio.

Big Close-Up (BCU)
This cuts off the top of the head and the bottom of the chin, but not the mouth. It is used rarely, usually at times of extreme tension or heightened emotion.

Close-Up (CU)
The head is in shot completely, the shot being cut off where the knot of a tie would be. Many people find this size shot uncomfortable, as it gives the impression of a floating head.

Medium Close-Up (MCU)
The most common shot on television. The top of the head is in shot, the shot is cut off at the top of a breast pocket. This shot size comfortably fills the 4 × 3 screen ratio.

Medium Shot (MS)
Also very common. The top of the head is in shot, the shot is cut off at the waist. Some countries find the MCU too close for comfort, and instead use the MS as the standard single shot.

Medium Long Shot (MLS)
Also sometimes known as a three-quarter shot, this is cut off at the knees. It is often used to set a presenter in context, i.e. with something in the background. Very common on single camera shoots for the 'piece to camera' at the end of news reports showing the reporter at the scene of the story.

Long Shot (LS)
The complete body is shown, normally with a little more headroom than foot room. Sometimes used for entrances and beginning of action, it tends to be a little too loose to use for too long.

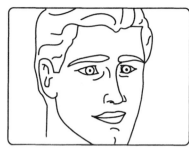

Big Close Up (BCU)

Close Up (CU)

Medium Close Up (CU)

Medium Shot or Mid Shot (MS)

Medium Long Shot (MLS)

Long Shot (LS)

Standard shots

Standard shots (2)

Semi Profile Shot
This is done either with the MCU or MS. The important points are to give enough 'looking room', i.e. that space on the side of the screen that the performer is looking towards, and to make sure that we can see both the eyes of the subject.

Profile Shot
This is more commonly known as 'a mistake'. Very occasionally it is a desirable effect, but few performers will thank you. The audience gets a perfect view of every bump and dent on the nose, combined with a great shot of the ear. We rarely see this view of people in real life as we tend to look straight on towards someone when having a conversation. If you do use this shot, you will need plenty of looking room.

Over the Shoulder (OTS)
Often used to see an actor's reaction to the person talking.

2-Shot (2S)
Fairly obviously two people in frame. The common mistake on a 2-shot is to have the people too far apart, leaving a big gap between them in the middle of the frame. News programmes with two seated presenters often position them uncomfortably close together to get a sensible-looking shot.

2-Shot Favouring Actor A (2S fav A)
Very common in situation comedy where you need to see both the person talking and a performer reacting to the statement. Often used by American directors in combination with a 2-shot favouring B, although some people find this a little too close to a jump cut.

Wide Angle (WA)
Used as a stage setter, you might be surprised to read this is shot using a wide angle lens. But then again, you might not.

Semi Profile

Profile

Over the shoulder

2-Shot

2-Shot Favouring Actor A

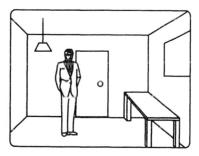

Wide Angle

Standard shots

Picture composition (1)

There is no complete set of rules for picture composition although there are a number of commonly-held views about well composed shots. If you freeze the playback of a programme at any point, you should see a still frame that looks good.

Know your monitor
Please make sure the monitor you are using to look at shots has been properly set up. Some monitors are over-scanned or under-scanned. Many show incorrect colours and a surprising number of television studios do not set up the brightness and contrast of monitors accurately.

Rule of thirds
Probably the best known starting point for composing a shot. If you divide the screen into thirds and place objects of interest at the intersection points then the image will usually look well composed.

This rule should not be slavishly followed, otherwise all the shots end up looking the same. However, it has worked for thousands of directors before, and will again.

Headroom
Please do not chop the tops off people's heads unless you really mean to. Give sufficient space so that heads do not look cramped at the top of the screen.

Looking room
Generally we give looking room in the direction the person is facing. Similarly if the person is running, we would give extra space in the direction they are travelling.

Centre framing
Probably the weakest place to put any object. While it is safe – if it moves a bit it is unlikely to go out of frame – it is definitely dull.

Balancing shots
If you are placing someone or something on one side of the screen, you will usually need something on the other side to balance up the picture. The obvious exception is where you want to show loneliness or desolation, in which case the empty space becomes integral to the composition.

Headroom can look very different from monitor to monitor, depending how they have been set up.

When balancing a picture don't let the background objects be too distracting – static objects generally work well.

It's also a useful way of placing your presenter in context – if they are at an art exhibition, show some artwork around them.

Keep an eye out for what's behind a presenter – try to prevent trees from growing out of heads, Mickey Mouse ears etc.

Centre framing is most useful in front of a locked off camera, or one being remotely controlled, when you need the extra safety margin in case the person moves at all.

33

Picture composition (2)

Background setting

Placing a person in an appropriate background can greatly affect their apparent integrity. Dress them in a white coat, put them in a laboratory and most people will believe they are intelligent and trustworthy.

Use of different focal lengths

You can change the perceived size of two people by changing the focal length of the lens.

If two people are in a scene together and you shoot them with a tight lens from a fair distance, they appear a similar size on screen. Alternatively, a wider lens can be used and the camera moved closer to the front performer. She is the same size on screen as before, but the background person now appears much smaller, or more distant.

Viewpoint

If we shoot from a low angle (LA) a person appears to become more powerful. Alternatively, if we shoot from a high angle (HA) they look smaller and diminished in stature.

When you have two performers together the angle of shot affects our relative perception. A high angle shot makes the background person appear stronger. In a low angle shot the foreground person appears to look down on the background person, giving strength to the actor nearest the camera.

Objects in a line

A mistake typical of new directors is putting all objects in one horizontal line instead of breaking them up. This is both visually dull, and, in human terms, unnatural behaviour.

Always remember you have three axis to play with, not just the horizontal (the x-axis) and vertical (the y-axis). The z-axis runs out of the television towards the viewer, and creating movement down this line can be dramatic and effective.

Putting actors in a straight line all facing forward is particularly common in low budget dramas and situation comedies. It's easy to shoot and get clean single shots, but it looks ridiculous.

Use of diagonals

For some reason humans find aesthetic beauty in non-horizontal lines. This is most apparent in ballet, where so much effort goes into choreographing positions to create lines and curves. On the television screen, diagonal and 'V' shaped lines create comfortable pleasing composition, whether it be a landscape or a movement.

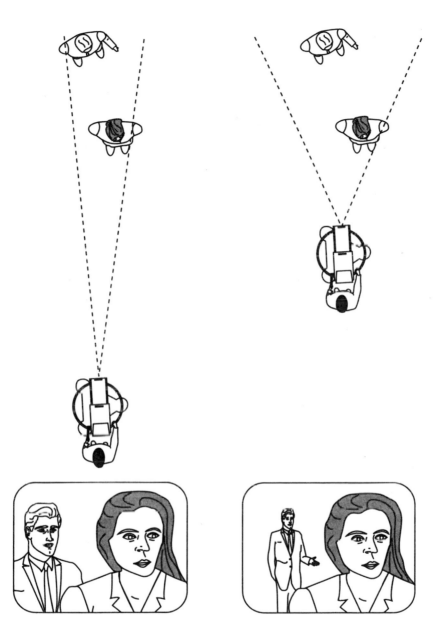

Adjusting background object size without changing foreground

Tracking and crabbing

Tracking is the physical movement of a camera towards and away from the principal subject. Crabbing is the sideways movement of a camera.

You cannot crab forwards or backwards. You cannot track left or right. Sorry, that's just the way it is. If you use the wrong terminology most camera crews will assume you are inexperienced.

Tracking and crabbing on a tight shot
Don't.

If you've ever tried looking through a strong set of binoculars you'll know that any hand shaking is exaggerated, and it's difficult to hold a steady picture. The same goes for television cameras. If you zoom in, then make the camera move, the slightest bump or imperfection on the floor will be screamingly obvious.

Arcing
This is a term that is going out of fashion but is a useful concept. The camera moves around the subject, but stays the same distance away (i.e. it travels a circular path, the centre point of which is the subject). This has the advantage that the focal distance will remain set correctly, but it is hard to move a ped in a constantly changing direction.

Using foreground
A common mistake inexperienced directors make when crabbing, tracking or craning is not having anything in the foreground. If all your subject is a long distance from the camera you will need to crab for ages to see any effect. If there is a foreground near the camera you can crab shorter and more slowly and get a stronger feeling from the shot.

Why crab, track and crane?

1. It can look great. There is something wonderfully expensive-looking about a well-designed and crafted tracking shot.
2. You can save having to use several shots by developing one instead.

Camera moves need to be motivated. This will usually be the action from the performers, although a camera movement in itself can create a feeling that subconsciously is passed on to the viewer. We get a strong feeling of speed if we are crabbing alongside someone running. If we crane up leaving an actor in the middle of an empty space we convey the feeling of them being left alone and lonely.

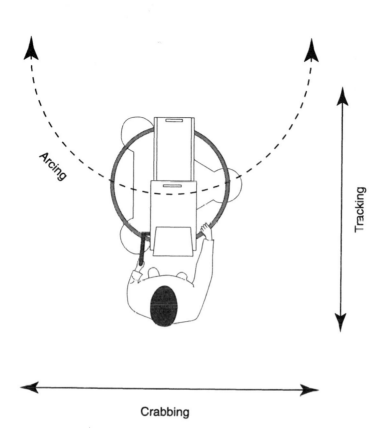

Arcing

Tracking

Crabbing

Crossing the line

The best known mistake, and one of the easiest to prevent in a multi-camera studio, is crossing the line.

Suppose we have two people talking to each other and you've placed the cameras as in the diagram. If we tried to cut the pictures together it would look like they are ignoring each other and speaking to outer space.

The line
There is an imaginary line that runs from the eyes of one person to the eyes of the other. This line extends to infinity in both directions.

If you keep all your cameras on the same side of the line you will not be crossing the line, and the shots will cut together.

This goes for objects, people, sports etc. If you covered a football match and had cameras down both sidelines, then one moment the home team would be attacking the goal to the left, the next they would be trying to score in the goal to the right. In this case the line is between the two goal mouths.

Neutral shots
Occasionally you need to be able to cross the line to get to action on the other side. The easiest methods are to throw in a neutral shot, or to travel across the line while on shot.

A neutral shot is either directly on the line, or perpendicular to it. There is a shot of a train, for example. The next shot is from front on, showing the train hurtling towards the viewers. The next shot can now be on the other side.

The perpendicular shot is normally from straight above. For example, in an interview a ceiling-mounted camera can give a top-down view. No matter which camera you are on you can always cut to this neutral shot and from that to any camera.

Breaking the rule
In fact, we cross the line more often than people realise. Usually it's not too noticeable if we use wide shots or a cut-away to mask the join.

The recovery
If you have shot across the line and are sitting in an edit suite with an editor who thinks you are a complete idiot for making such an elementary mistake, try flipping the picture on the x-axis (i.e. mirror it). As long as there is nothing too obvious in the background (like writing) you might get away with it for a brief shot.

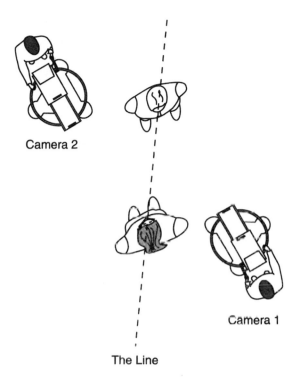

Camera 2

Camera 1

The Line

Camera 1

Camera 2

Camera commands

The reason for having standard instructions in a control room has nothing to do with being pedantic. It is simply the fastest, most accurate way for directors to get what they want.

Planned camera commands

These are the instructions written onto scripts and camera cards. They are the shots and movements we have detailed already, and will be immediately understood by all professional camera operators. The table opposite shows a summary.

Unplanned commands

These are used to adjust the shots to the director's liking. Always be aware that while you can see what all the cameras are offering, they can only see their own picture (although experienced operators will have a good idea of what the others are shooting). Shots will invariably need to be adjusted, particularly when you are matching shots from two cameras.

The commands are the same as for planned ones, but try to quantify the adjustment. If you tell a camera to pan right, they will have no idea where you want them to stop. Try instead to use expressions like 'Pan right until the door is completely in frame'.

Do not just say 'Camera 2, looking room'. An operator will not know whether that means you want more of it or less – be specific.

It's a nice touch if you can remember the names of the camera operators. Big stickers under the camera monitors make this a lot easier, but do not jeopardise the production for this nicety. If there are two operators with the same name, you must call both cameras by their numbers. When you are live and it gets very busy it is easier to call numbers, and all crews will understand if you revert to camera numbers when it gets hectic.

Crashing in or out

Usually in a fast-moving programme the camera operators will assume the vision mixer may cut to them with little or no warning. Consequently they may move to a shot more slowly than they need to, so that it could at least look like a deliberate shot if it was cut to air.

There are times when you need a shot as fast as is possible. If you say to a camera operator 'Crash to a single', it means that they can zoom in very fast, and you will not cut to it until it has arrived. Vision mixers should also understand it to mean 'Do not cut to the camera until it has arrived, but take it as soon as possible'.

Script	Command
BCU	Big Close-Up
CU/CS	Close-Up/Close Shot
MCU	Medium Close-Up
MS	Mid Shot
MLS	Medium Long Shot
LS	Long shot
VLS	Very Long Shot
WA	Wide Angle
LA/HA	Low Angle/High Angle
2S	2-Shot
OTS, O/S	Over the Shoulder
C, COF	Centre/Centre of Frame
Z/I, Z/O	Zoom in/Zoom out
fav	FAVouring
fr L or R	FRame Left or Right
A/B	As Before
Also:	Pan L or R
	Tilt up or down
	Ped up/elevate
	Ped down/depress
	Crane up or down
	Crab L or R
	Arc L or R
	Track in or out
	Focus up/defocus/pull focus

Camera commands – summary

Wardrobe

This is not just the ironing and cleaning department. They have technical knowledge of television clothing, and the artistic ability to interpret briefs from directors. Properly-designed clothes will allow for the performer's movement and be made to last as long as required.

Wardrobe departments also take into account cultural sensibilities and transmission times (you may be permitted to use more revealing clothes very late at night which would be unsuitable for a family audience).

Technical issues

White shirts and some light pastels are too white and will 'burn-out', losing all details. Instead we use 'television white', which is slightly grey or cream, but appears as white on camera.

Similarly black velvet is too black, so wardrobe departments use a 'television black', which is actually slightly grey.

Herringbone and small checks are a nightmare. They appear to 'strobe' on camera and look dreadful because of the way colour information is coded into a television signal. They must be avoided if at all possible.

Strapless dresses can look strange. A medium close-up shot shows the head and bare shoulders. Without being able to see the dress it looks like the subject is naked.

Jewellery can be noisy, especially for personal mics which tend to be fitted exactly where necklaces lie. It can also be very reflective and distracting, which can dominate a picture.

What wardrobe want to know from you

They need to know the programme content and style. Drama directors need to detail the characters, along with the period and the place where the story occurs. For non-dramas, is the show relaxed (jeans and sweat shirts) or formal (suits and power clothing)? Do you intend to use chroma-key, in which case what colour?

The clothes sizes of your presenters should be given in plenty of time, including shoe and hat sizes.

Planning for a rainy day

Presenters who might have to appear on screen at short notice should have a full set of clean clothes permanently available at the studio. For newsreaders this should include dark and sober clothes in case they have to make announcements of national interest (death of a prime minister etc.).

Given sufficient information, time and budget, wardrobe departments will offer a range of outfits to suit your programme requirements.

Even straightforward shows may need extensive wardrobe assistance. For example, a quiz show with one host and hostess may have a policy of not using the same clothes on more than one show in a series. If five programmes are being recorded each day for two weeks, then 50 outfits for each presenter will be required, plus a couple of spares.

Make-up

Contrary to popular belief the function of make-up is not just to make people look as good as possible in front of the camera. The aim is to get quality pictures from your studio, and to assist performers in their roles. Make-up can normally be considered in one of three groups.

Straight

This doesn't greatly change the appearance of the presenter or performer, but compensates for the environment we work in – namely under hot lights for a long period. Typically this includes removing 'shine' from foreheads, lightening bags under eyes and strengthening lips. It also includes reducing blotchy skin and darkening pale faces.

Corrective

This sorts out 'problems' with appearance. It includes covering up scar tissue, skin blemishes, growths and thinning hair. The aim here is to improve appearance without giving the impression of being made up.

Character

This assists the portrayal of the character, and is used extensively in drama. It can be facial reshaping, changing hair etc., right the way up to creating monsters. Specialists may be brought in for prosthetics to build up the skin and add body parts. Complex hair and wigs are also usually done by an expert in this field.

Planning and staffing

In preparing for a programme you need to make sure there are enough make-up facilities to cope with your requirements. The floor manager should make sure your contributors all get to make-up in time for your studio schedule.

For difficult make-up, which can take several hours in extreme cases, schedule sufficient time for the work to be done. You may have to plan your recording to use these performers late in the day.

Refurbishing

Most make-up wears off after a while, or the effect is reduced. It is useful to have a make-up artist in the studio keeping an eye on the state of the performers throughout the shoot. If not, then you must keep an eye on what the presenters look like yourself. Under the pressure to get a programme through a studio on time it's easy not to notice hair out of place, running make-up etc.

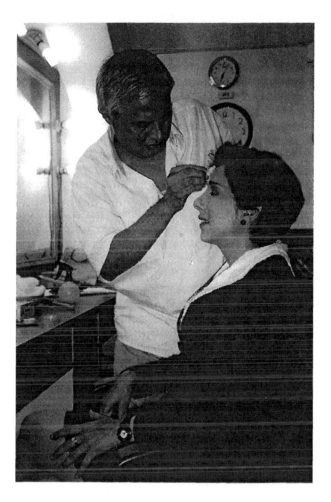

Courtesy New Delhi Television

The make-up artist is a bit of a cosmetic doctor, making people look better when they need help, and knowing the deepest secrets of the presenter's appearance (including any assistance they may be using to retain a youthful look).

Some presenters only feel comfortable working with their regular make-up artists, who know not only what is needed of their craft skills, but also have the temperament to deal with performers' tensions and personalities.

Seating plans

This comes under the 'dull but necessary' category of the director's work. One person (normally the director) needs to decide where each guest is to sit. This information is distributed in a simple form that everyone will understand. Do not make it more complicated than it needs to be.

The floor manager will make sure the guests have arrived, gone through make-up and are sitting on the right seat in time for the planned slot. If they are not going to be ready (e.g. guest fails to arrive) the FM should let you know in sufficient time for you to make alternative arrangements.

The sound team will usually want to mark up microphone channels on the sound desk with the name of the guests.

Vision mixers find it useful to have a seating plan so that they can cut to the correct person during an introduction. It also gives them more confidence when captioning people to know for certain who they are.

Editorial considerations

Deciding who should sit where is not as straightforward as simply filling in holes on a seating plan. You should understand which of the visitors is most important to the story. Is there a danger of one guest overshadowing another? You may want to place the more fragile person near the centre of the set. Who disagrees with whom? Do you need to have a physical barrier between two people? (I'm thinking of a table here, rather than barbed wire.)

Greeters and green rooms

Some programmes with many guests appearing each day have professional greeters. They make sure the guests are comfortable while waiting to go to make-up or the studio.

Traditionally the room guests relax in is the 'green room'. I've no idea where the name came from, but I'm sure one day a smug old person who has been working in television since John Logie Baird first declared 'This picture is non-sync' will tell me.

Making guests comfortable has a couple of advantages. It improves their on-camera performance and you are more likely to get stars to come back again if you treat them well.

In lower budget programmes, or in shows with few guests, the job of greeting guests often falls to someone on the production team. It may be inconvenient for someone to take the time to look after a nervous visitor, but it needs to be done, and it needs to be done well.

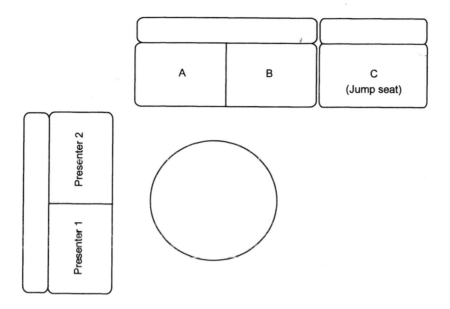

	A	B	C (Jump seat)

Presenter 2

Presenter 1

| Presenter 1: Anita Scanlon | | | |
| Presenter 2: Mark Spudlove | | | |

Time	Seat A	Seat B	Seat C
0615	Dr Stock		
0630	Peter Ordinaire	Jo Ordinaire	
0645	Andrew Sport		
0715	Helen Citizen	Mungo Citizen	Kylie Citizen
0730	Henry Zodiac		

Seating plan for breakfast television programme

The floor plan

This is used by set designers and constructors to make sure they're building the set you want and putting it in the right place. For many regular programmes you may never see the floor plan, particularly if you are using a permanent set.

Corrections are cheap – for now
The whole point of plans is to catch problems before it's too late. It is important that you go through the various shots you intend to use, and see if they will work (size, background etc.).

If you need something to change it is easier for a designer to come up with alternatives at this stage. Waiting until the set is in the studio makes alterations expensive and time-consuming.

If the plan is complex, some studios like to make up a three-dimensional model of the set. This helps many people visualise what the final studio will look like, particularly those who don't regularly work off floor plans.

Scale
The significance of scale is not just so that you can work out the size everything needs to be to fit. It also allows you to check the shots you intend to use before the set is made.

Using a basic protractor you can draw simple angles from your various camera points and see which parts of the set will appear in shot.

Camera positions
Once a floor plan is finalised the director normally gets a copy upon which he works out the various camera positions. Traditionally these are drawn by a circle with a nose. Inside the circle you write the camera and position number. You end up with a series of circles for each camera, marked 1A, 1B, 1C etc. (for camera 1), in shot positions A, B and C.

Other users
The floor plan is also used by the lighting director, who works out which lights are to be used from which points. The sound supervisor may also use a copy of the completed layout to plan which wall boxes are to be used for the various microphones, talkback lines etc.

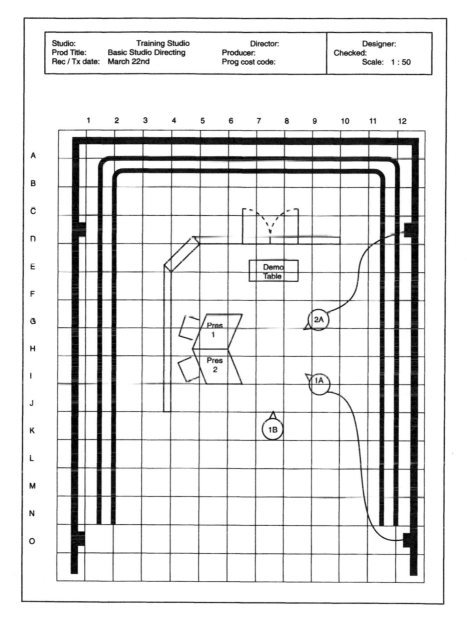

Studio: Training Studio
Prod Title: Basic Studio Directing
Rec / Tx date: March 22nd

Director:
Producer:
Prog cost code:

Designer:
Checked:
Scale: 1 : 50

Demo
Table

Pres
1

Pres
2

2A

1A

1B

Basic floor plan for a simple set

Positioning cameras

From your floor plan you should have a good idea how many cameras you will need in each area of the studio. If you are working on a programme that has been running for some time, this will have been done already, and it is usually worth fitting in with the camera positions and numbers that are familiar to everyone else.

Cable runs

Most studios have a number of wall boxes that cameras can plug into. You will have to consider lengths of cables available as well as where the cables will lie during your shoot in deciding which wall boxes to use (i.e. will a cable appear in shot dragged across the centre of your stage?).

Crossing cameras

While it is possible to direct cameras across the front of each other, there are two obvious dangers.

If the camera in front doesn't fully clear the second camera's shot, you lose a camera until it has moved sufficiently out of the way. Additionally cables can become tangled, with some cameras sitting inside other operators' 'loops'.

Reverse numbering

While it might seem obvious to lay out the cameras from left to right, there is something to be said for reversing this order.

Suppose you have an interview with two cameras. If you lay them out left to right, the view in the monitor stack is of two people looking away from each other. However, if you put camera 2 to the left of camera 1, then in the control room the two people appear to be talking to each other. Many new directors find this arrangement more natural.

Set limitations

Studio sets are not normally designed to carry heavy weights. A full camera pedestal with camera, lens and prompter unit is more than enough to overload lightweight flooring, so if you need to have cameras inside your set you will have to consider using lightweight tri-pods and smaller camera/lens combinations.

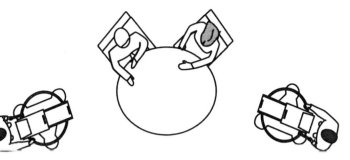

Camera 1   Camera 2

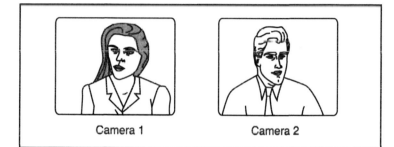

Camera 1   Camera 2

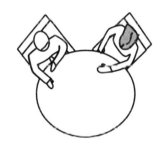

Camera 2   Camera 1

Camera 1   Camera 2

51

Monitor stacks

It is not unusual to walk into a control room and see 60 monitors in a stack. While this may appear daunting, the stack is there for your benefit and, used effectively, it helps prevent problems getting to air.

Layout of monitors

There are thousands of ways you can lay out monitors in a control room, so I cannot give the definitive description here. However, there are some basic layout rules used by most designers.

The transmission monitor should be the biggest, right in the middle. If the picture is wrong here, it will be wrong on your recording or live transmission. Right next to it is the preview monitor. The vision mixer should always put the next source on this monitor, and as a director you must notice what is there. If it is incorrect, say so.

Most sources are grouped together (cameras, VTs, graphics etc.). Become familiar where the groups are in your stack.

Outside source lines (they may be called something else in your studio, but they are for outside broadcasts, satellite feeds etc.) should be visible the whole time. Note that just because you can see someone on an outside source line it does not mean the line is ready or able to be used.

There should be a monitor so that you can see what captions keyed over the output will look like (usually the DSK, or downstream key preview). You must get in the habit of checking this before telling the vision mixer to super.

The mixed effects previews are for the vision mixer to prepare more complicated set-ups.

There should be a prompter monitor in the control room so that you know if the presenter is seeing the correct story. Use it and check it regularly.

If your studio is to go live you will need an 'off-air' monitor. **Warning**: If your off-air monitor shows a breakdown while you are live it doesn't necessarily mean the studio output is not getting to air in other parts of the country (it may be a regional transmission problem). Do not stop your programme until you have been told to do so by presentation.

Tally lights

Many studios have a system of red tally lights that appear under the monitors of the sources that are on-air, as well as on the cameras themselves. This is particularly useful when shooting an interview, as you will probably spend the bulk of your time looking at the camera monitors, not the transmission monitor.

News control rooms can be enormous. Initially this can put many directors off, but with time you will find all of those monitors useful. Their primary function is to let you see all the incoming sources, while also showing you what is available at what point on the vision mixer.

The largest studios often have the smallest monitor stacks, on the basis that they are probably used mainly for large dramas, which do not involve complex live operations. Usually you just need to see the cameras, and a couple of VTs.

Vision mixers

The vision mixer (or switcher) is both the name of the machine and the job title of the person operating it. This section is about the machine. Many places expect directors to be able to vision mix at the same time. There is a big clue here ... if you want to survive long term as a director, use every chance to learn and develop your vision-mixing skills.

Capabilities
All vision mixers are capable of the same basic functions – cutting, mixing, wiping and keying. Different manufacturers use different layouts and terms for some functions, and larger machines have extensive memories for storing complex composites.

Cut, mix
Ninety-five per cent of television is cutting and mixing between two sources. This is done between two 'buses', which simply means two rows of buttons.

The 'program bus' is the on-air row, so any source selected here is instantly cut to air. The program monitor shows the program bus output.

The 'preview bus' is where the vision mixer pre-selects the next source to go on air, and it appear on the preview monitor. Both of you can now easily see and check the next source or shot. You will always have a preview monitor in front of you – **use it**!

Wipes
Basic wipes are simple to do on all vision mixers. Some machines have a huge selection of built-in wipe patterns, others have only a limited selection. Find out what your equipment can do.

Most wipes can have a border, with a colour of your choice. There is a temptation to use bright, thick borders which should be resisted unless they really suit the style of the programme. Bear in mind that your work is probably being recorded, and your lack of good taste may come back to haunt you in years to come.

The speed of mixes and wipes is described in frames, so a one-second duration mix is 25 frames (PAL) or 30 frames (NTSC).

Mix effects (M/E)
Most vision mixers have between one and three 'mix effects' banks. This is what makes the machine look so complicated, with dozens of buttons. They are really just sub-mixers, where wipes, mixes etc. can be set up and checked in advance, then put on-air at the touch of one button.

Key bus and downstream keyer (DSK)
Vision mixers can select a range of sources to be keyed. The most common will be caption generators and digital video effects.

Large mixers are needed for programmes with many sources (e.g. news, large sports outside broadcasts), or where many key layers are needed (lots of captions/graphics/ digital video effects). They are very flexible which is why they are installed in many studios, even though rarely will all the buttons be used in anger.

Small vision mixers are usually capable of mixing/cutting/wiping between eight sources and adding captions.

This covers at least 90 per cent of television and all directors should be able to operate this level of machine.

Caption generators

Captioning people and information is editorially vital. If you do not know who the interviewee is and what they do, you cannot judge whether they are talking from a neutral standpoint, or have a vested self interest.

While it is possible to put captions on VT in some edit suites, there are a couple of advantages in doing all captioning through the studio. You don't need to pay for captioning equipment in every edit suite, and it is easier to ensure the same format or house style (font, size, layout etc.) is followed.

If you are working on a long-running programme then chances are someone has already set up the format for captions. Learn what the standard layouts are, and whether capital letters should be used for names or titles. House style includes the transition to captions, i.e. mix in and mix out, or cut in, mix out etc.

There is a temptation to throw captions up as soon as you see someone being interviewed. **Wait until they actually answer the question.** The exception is if you need to put up a series of translation captions, in which case you may have a large number to get through in a short time.

Leave captions on screen long enough for the viewers to read. A useful technique is for you to read them off your output monitor twice before taking the caption out.

Types of caption generators

There are many manufacturers of captioning equipment, which unfortunately has led to numerous different commands from directors as there is a tendency to refer to the machine manufacturer rather than the generic term.

Aston, Chyron, and Dubner are some of the terms you may hear, although it makes far more sense for everyone to refer to 'capgen' in all instructions. This is particularly the case as more and more caption generators are PC-based, using software from one manufacturer and specialist hardware from another.

Shadows and surrounds

Apart from changing the font and size of text, it is easy to alter the appearance of text by using shadows and surrounds. Note that the vision mixer needs to be equipped with a linear keyer if you want soft edges or translucent backgrounds.

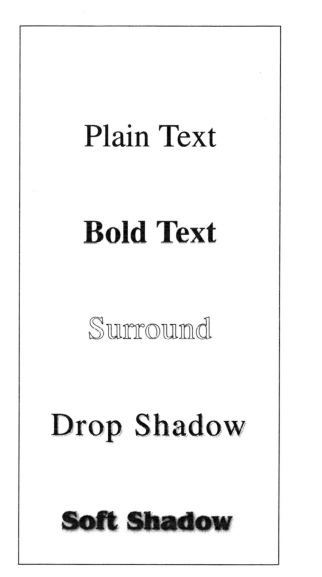

The choice of caption style includes the font, size, colour, shadows (drop/soft) and background (should the words sit on a translucent strip?).

Not all vision mixers or caption generators are capable of giving you all of these options.

Keying

Mixing to a caption doesn't work
First let's clarify why we need to key at all. Suppose you have a white caption on a black background. You want to superimpose this over a general view. If we try just mixing the two together, the background picture dims and the caption doesn't fully come through.

Adding a caption to a background picture
The next logical thing to do is to add a caption to the background picture. That would be fine if all of the background picture was dark, but if you added a white caption to a bright background, you would quickly end up with an illegal signal that is way too bright.

Cutting a hole
The way we get around the problem is to cut a hole in the background picture first, then fill it with the video from the caption generator. That's fine, if you have white text on a black background. It would be easy to use the white signal to cut the hole, but what if you want to use black text?

The solution is for the caption generator to send two signals. One, the video fill, is the picture as the caption will appear on screen. The second, the video key signal, tells the vision mixer the exact shape of the caption.

Shadows
One benefit of this key (or 'matte') signal is that we can use it to create shadows of the text. If the key signal is wider than the text, we get a border around the text on screen. We use the same idea to create drop shadows.

Soft shadows
We can also use the key signal to generate soft edges. If, instead of sending a solid key signal, we send a mid level, or grey key signal, the vision mixer will interpret that as a half mix of that part of the caption. We can use this technique to create solid captions over soft, translucent backgrounds.

Self keying
Occasionally we don't want to use the key signal. For example, suppose you have a full frame logo going into your DVE. If you want to place that on a background picture, you wouldn't want the solid box from the DVE. Instead you would want to keep the bright parts of the picture, i.e. key off the video coming out of the DVE, not from the DVE key signal.

(A) The background picture

(B) The capgen video fill. The toxt wo have decided to use is mostly black, but has been bevel shaped.

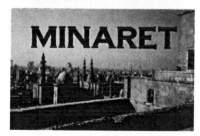

(C) The capgen video key. This shows the exact shape we want the lettering to appear on the final composite.

(D) The hole has been cut using (C) as a template.

(E) The video fill (B) is added into the hole cut by the key signal.

59

Digital video effects (static)

Most middle to large scale studios and many editing suites have digital video effects (DVE) devices. Non-linear machines often have built-in DVE software.

Capabilities

DVEs can physically move the picture around the screen, whereas a wipe on a vision mixer can only select parts of a picture in its current position. DVEs can usually shrink, rotate, skew, move, bend and distort pictures. They can be programmed to animate between positions (often called keyframes).

To do this each frame has to be loaded into a memory, then read out in its new position on the screen. This means there is a slight delay through a DVE – normally one frame.

This is not normally enough to give lip-sync problems, but it can do if combined with other synchronisers/frame stores.

DVE as a positioner

Most audiences know we can fly a picture around the screen. Most audiences are no longer impressed, so now we don't normally bother.

The main use of DVEs tends to be as a positioner, and the obvious example is when you have an interview between two locations, and you want to see both sources at the same time. While it's easy to program the DVE to animate the pictures back and forward, current thinking tends towards straight cutting, as being sharper and less intrusive.

Two 4 × 3 pictures do not fit on a screen very well (they tend to come out both very small), so often one of the images is cropped (i.e. wiped out), changing the aspect ratio. In the illustration the studio shot has been severely cropped, but the final image sizes are quite large.

Always let camera operators know if you will be cropping their shot. Ideally they should be able to preview the effect, but this may not always be possible.

Many people use the two-way boxes to remind the audience of the location of the pictures. If the pictures are live, this is also usually rammed down the viewers' throats.

The dual channel DVE (i.e. it can work on two moving sources at the same time) has been used to crop the sides off the newsroom shot, and to place the two pictures over a graphic stills store background. Both boxes can normally be done with a single keyer.

Typically this shot follows the two-way boxes – the outside source with a caption identifying the contributor, using a second keyer.

Once the name is established, the capgen is mixed off leaving a logo or 'live flag' which needs a third keyer.

Digital video effects (moving)

DVE moves

As a director you obviously need to be clear what you want the DVE move to do, and to explain that to the vision mixer. Give them time to program up the device, and check any move when it is finished.

During the recording use one standard expression to let the vision mixer know when you want any animation to happen. There is a tendency to use the name of the device, but there are dozens of different DVE makers, and they change every few years. It is better to say 'Animate' or 'DVE'.

Special effects

There are occasions when DVEs are used to create a special effect, either in the way they move the picture or distort the video signal. Wobbly pictures indicating a dream sequence are part of most people's visual vocabulary. Posterisation distorts the video signal, inverting colour and luminance information, and is still commonly built into DVEs, although I don't know why because it is used very rarely.

Filters

As non-linear devices become more common in both post-production suites and in studios for replaying pre-edited sequences, the crossover between electronic filters and DVEs is becoming blurred.

Software for manipulating still images in computers developed what they called filters – often 'plug-ins' that could be bought from independent programmers. While they started as fairly simple devices to mimic lens filters, they grew to become mini applications in their own right, and are now capable of serious image manipulation.

These same filters could also be applied to moving images, which are, after all, just a sequence of still pictures. It took some time, as each picture had to be loaded, filtered and re-saved. As hardware speeds and parallel processing developed, computers were able to apply filters in real time – which is effectively what a DVE device does.

So in the future we can expect DVEs to be able to achieve many of the picture manipulations currrently being done on still images.

Original picture

Picture with texturising video effect applied

Electronic filters, currently used in post-production and non-linear editing systems, should be built into digital video effects devices of the future.

Graphics

Graphics departments used to be concerned with static images, but that is no longer the case. However, one of the most common devices you will come across is a stills store.

Stacks

A programme that requires a lot of graphics will usually have them prepared beforehand and built into a stack – i.e. a list of the graphics in the order they need to appear on screen is programmed into the stills store.

Most stills stores give you two outputs (or 'channels'), which function according to the type of stack you have prepared. Both channels usually appear on the vision mixer, although some small studios only use one.

Programme/preview

Here you use one of the output channels for cutting the pictures to air (i.e. the 'programme' channel) while the preview channel shows the next graphic in your stack. If you need to go straight from one graphic to the next, the operator can change down from the preview to the programme channel.

For a director this is nice and easy. You always know where the output channel is, and you can see the next graphic. The down side is that there are very few transitions that can be carried out by the graphics operators to go between two stills.

A/B stack

In this mode of operation, the graphics will appear alternately on channel A then channel B. Slightly harder for a director, you have to be thoroughly aware which channel your next graphic is lined up on, as you will have to call to the VM which channel you want cut to air.

It is bad practice to tell the VM to take graphics without specifying which channel, and usually shows that the director has lost track of his sources.

You can now perform any transition you like between the sources, as the transition is being done through your vision mixer.

Moving sources

Some graphics departments have the ability to play animations straight to air (e.g. Quantel's 'Harry'). As a director, be very specific what source you want the vision mixer to use next; 'Coming to Harry 1 on a mix … and mix, animate Harry'.

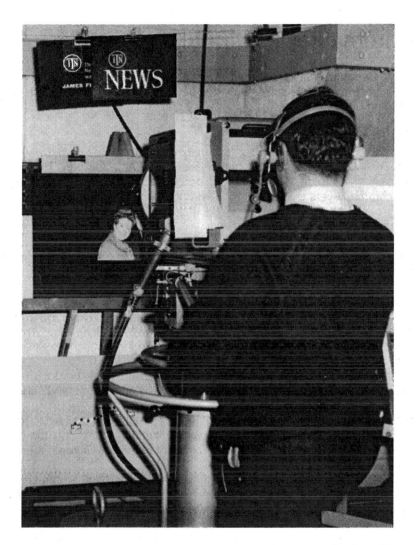

All television graphics including captions used to be done with hard copies placed in front of cameras.
Animating graphics meant someone pushing bits of card around in front of a background.

Chroma-keying/virtual studios

We've been using blue (or green) screen in film and television for a number of years. There are a few technical details you have to consider in your planning.

Why use blue?
The choice of blue as a colour is simply because there is relatively little blue in the reflectance of any human skin tone. And you don't get many people with blue hair. Technically we don't need to use blue – most modern chroma-keyers are capable of keying out any colour.

What happens?
The vision mixer looks at the signal as it comes in. Wherever it sees blue, it takes that bit out and replaces it with another video source. We are not talking brain surgery here.

Standard mistakes
Obviously the presenters' clothes cannot contain the background colour. This includes gentlemen's ties. The real difficulty is getting even lighting across the whole blue section, without getting too much blue light reflected onto the foreground.

Panning or zooming the foreground camera should only be done if that really is the effect you want. The background will appear to stand still.

How does chroma-keying differ from a virtual studio?
Virtual studios use chroma-keying, but additionally if you pan the foreground camera (the one with a person in front of the blue screen) then the background moves as well.

This is a substantially harder engineering trick than plain chroma-keying. For the background to move in a matched manner it has to be generated by a computer. That computer has to know the exact focal length of the lens on the foreground camera, its position on the floor, its height, when it is panning, how fast etc. It then has to calculate the theoretical background, up to thirty times a second.

Courtesy ITN

Judicious use of chroma-keying can make even the smallest studio turn out an expensive-looking product. You do need sufficient space to light the background evenly without reflecting too much colour onto the foreground subject.

Cutting cameras

The following are general rules and classic television theory. It doesn't mean you can't break them, but you should know and understand the rules first, and break them for good reasons.

Most cutting is obvious, and there is a danger of over-intellectualising it instead of simply cutting when your gut instinct tells you to. The main point is that cuts should be motivated. This motivation might come visually from inside the frame, from sound or from the dramatic content.

Visual motivation

You have a wide shot of a set at the beginning of a scene (sometimes called the scene setter). A door opens. Cut to the door. This is a clear visual motivation. Who is coming through the door? Is he being inquisitive? Is he sneaking in or is it a flamboyant entrance?

Sound motivation

There is nothing worse than having a noise on television that is unexplained. If it is a background noise, particularly one that interferes with the main sound source, we need to see it to make sense of it. This is less of a problem in a soundproofed studio than on an external shoot, where you might not realise a cottage is next to a railway line and the sudden noise of an express train will not make any sense.

Dramatic motivation

This is a huge subject that could fill a book in its own right. The main point I want to make is that while the viewer usually wants to see the person talking, sometimes it is more important to see a person who is affected by what is being said. For example, if a character in a play is being told of an accident involving their child, the dramatic impact is clearly from the person receiving the news, not the messenger.

Cutting rules (classic)

Aim not to cut to or from a shot that is moving, i.e. cut, pan, stop, cut (this includes tilts and zooms). Within the shot the camera movement itself should be motivated (usually by the action of the performers).

Avoid cutting between two cameras offering similar shots.

If you are cross-cutting, match the camera shots up (similar size, looking room, headroom etc).

If you cut too quickly it can look like a mistake. Let the viewers take in your pictures.

Angle difference

Size difference

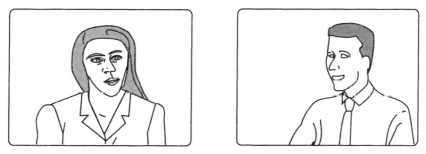

Looking room difference

Some examples of non-matching shots

69

The vision mixer (the operator)

If the vision mixer presses the wrong button, it is on air and cannot be salvaged. Needless to say, a good vision mixer is a vital member of the team.

Cutting and mixing

Vision mixers want to know clearly and simply what to take next and when, so develop the habit of clear speech patterns.

'Coming to 3 … and cut'
'Coming to VT 4 … VT 4 roll … and cut'.
'Coming to stills store A on a mix … and mix'.

Do not snap your fingers

This is an irritating habit for everybody on talkback, particularly the vision mixer, as it is impossible to react instantaneously to a snap. If you find yourself doing it unconsciously, hold a pencil in your hand.

Wipes

It is very hard to perform a smooth wipe manually, so they need to be automated – i.e. the vision mixer hits a button and the wipe takes as long as has been programmed into the machine. So the director must inform the vision mixer beforehand how quick they want the wipe to be. Smooth mixes can, however, be manually controlled by the vision mixer.

Keying

This primarily consists of putting captions on air. Use generic terms, not machine specific.

'Coming to capgen … and super.'

Preview

Your vision mixer should whenever possible put the next source on the preview monitor. Some prefer not to, but this should not be tolerated. If the wrong source is on preview, you have a chance of stopping an impending mistake. The exception to this is very fast sequences, like interviews, where 'hot cutting' is permissible.

Taking responsibility

If you as a director say, cut', it means you are happy for the picture on the preview monitor to go to air. If it is wrong, get it changed first.

It is your fault if you say 'cut' and the incorrect source on preview goes to air – you must take responsibility for that mistake.

Marked on Script:	Instruction
X	Mix
/	Cut
W	Wipe
CG, CAP	Caption Generator
S/I	Super (impose)
T/O	Take Out
Q, DVE, ADO, DPM, A-53, (and a few dozen others)	Animate Digital Video Effects
Also:	Animate (DVE)
	Change (Capgen or graphics)

Vision mixing commands

TJ	Telejector (gives a TV picture from a transparency)
TK	Telecine (replay off film)

Old sources, rarely used

The production assistant (PA)

The role of the production assistant (sometimes known as a 'timer' or 'director's assistant') varies from company to company, and programme to programme. I want to concentrate on the studio role, and in particular on how to make programmes run to time.

Stopwatch junkies

PAs have a counting fixation. Usually backwards. They count programmes on and off air. They count through VTs, letting everyone know when they are coming to an end. At some stations they count to the capgens that have to be added (assuming they have been given the information in the first place). During pre-planned sequences they will call out the shot numbers and which camera is next.

A few places make the PA run the VTs – although it is more common for the PA to give the VT a standby and for the director to roll the tape. Where the remote controls of VTs are fed into the control rooms (e.g. Betacart, Profile etc.) there seems to be a fairly even split between the number of people who make the PA roll the tapes, and those who make the director press the buttons.

Story durations

PAs work from information given to them. If they get fed duff information, then all their calculations will be wrong.

Awareness of timings

Directors must know whether programmes are running on time, as it is likely to hit you right between the eyeballs if you have to lose 30 seconds of time suddenly (i.e. crash out of a VT early or drop large chunks of the script). Programme editors will also need to be kept regularly up to date.

If you've just had a hectic sequence and finally run a VT of a couple of minutes duration, the PA will work out the overall calculations as soon as possible, but they need a few seconds. There is no point in demanding the answer as soon as you have cut to the VT – just wait a few moments.

Be clear how the end of the programme works, and talk to the PA beforehand to agree who is running what and when. You don't want to wait until 30 seconds to off air to discuss which of you was meant to run the capgen roller.

Out words

PAs should say what the out words of a VT are just before it finishes. They may sign 'Sign off' (SO) or 'Standard out cue' (SOQ), which means the standard phrase used by all reporters for that programme (e.g. John Martin, News at Eight').

Presenter into VT

```
         0                    16                        1.20
Vision   |    Presenter       |         VT                |

Sound    |    Link            |         SOT               |
```

Total dur = Link dur + VT dur.
E.g. Link = 16 sec, VT = 1:04, Tot dur = 1.20

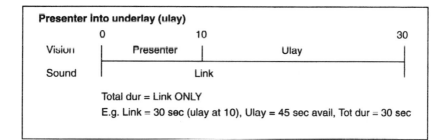

Presenter into underlay (ulay)

```
        0                 10                            30
Vision  |    Presenter     |           Ulay             |

Sound   |                Link                           |
```

Total dur = Link ONLY
E.g. Link = 30 sec (ulay at 10), Ulay = 45 sec avail, Tot dur = 30 sec

---

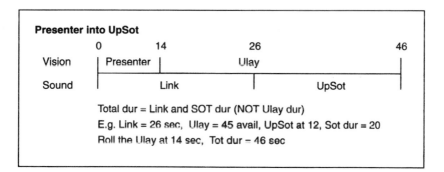

Presenter into UpSot

```
        0        14              26                46
Vision  | Presenter |         Ulay                  |

Sound   |        Link           |      UpSot         |
```

Total dur = Link and SOT dur (NOT Ulay dur)
E.g. Link = 26 sec, Ulay = 45 avail, UpSot at 12, Sot dur = 20
Roll the Ulay at 14 sec, Tot dur = 46 sec

Calculating durations of simple stories

The floor manager (FM)

The role of the floor manager varies depending on the type of production, but for the purposes of this book I will restrict myself to their work in the studio.

Safety
The FM is responsible for safety on the studio floor. That means they have the authority to stop a production if they are unhappy with the safety arrangements for a show.

They are responsible for the presence and use of all substances in the studio, including glass, pyrotechnics and aerosols. This is particularly important when working with a studio audience, or with young or disabled people.

Interpret and relay instructions from the control room
This may not be necessary if the presenters are on talkback, but even so the FM checks that the presenters heard the instructions.

The 'interpreting' bit is important. There are many times when the control room has become very stressful, and the FM has interpreted 'Get the ******* presenter onto the stage now' into 'We'd like to start recording please Mr Entertainment. So, starting positions everyone ....'

Cue presenters
They make sure the presenters know which camera they are working to, and they give countdowns in the studio for everyone not on talkback.

Co-ordinate props, sets and wardrobe
During small programmes they take care of props etc. On larger programmes they either work with assistant floor managers (AFM), or with specialist prop, set and wardrobe staff.

Anticipate problems
An experienced FM will predict problems before they happen, and will probably sort them out before you even know they exist.

'Mr Good-vibes'
The hardest part of the job to teach, and the bit everyone appreciates most, is the influence on staff morale. Studio days can be long. People can become stressed. An FM can absorb much of the pressure as it builds up, and protect the innocent from a tirade of abuse. The FM looks after everybody.

Nobody looks after the FM.

The floor manager is the director on the floor. Expected to be permanently full of energy, they should take much of the pressure off the director.

Studio sound

The sound department provide the technical and artistic recording of your programme sound from the studio floor. This may be in mono or stereo.

They replay into the studio pre-recorded music and effects as required by the production. They look after talkback and communications. They normally provide radio talkback units for production/sound/lighting. They are usually ignored far too much of the time. Sorry guys.

The sound team

The sound supervisor mixes all the sources on the sound desk. He may have one or more assistants, depending on the size and nature of the programme.

On the studio floor a sound assistant may either operate a boom (for sitcoms, dramas) or make sure all guests are fitted with microphones for interview programmes.

There may be another assistant in the sound room either looking after the communications, or assisting with the replay of audio tapes, grams, mini-disks etc.

Sound and pictures

The sound room will normally have a mini monitor stack. This shows them what is on air and what is on pre-set (i.e. the next shot you will cut to). Additionally they may have monitors for each of the VT machines and the outside sources (OS).

Stereo

More and more programmes are being recorded in stereo. While this adds an obvious technical complexity to the rigging and mixing of the show, there are some artistic questions that affect the director.

Suppose you are recording an orchestra. The violins are on the left, the cellos and double basses on the right. The sound supervisor places those instruments appropriately in the left and right stereo channels. If you cut to a camera at the back of the orchestra, should the sound reverse?

Technical information

As a director you may well be aware of specific information about the way VTs have had their audio tracks laid. Most VTs are recorded with two audio tracks – the standard formats are shown in the diagram opposite.

Mono	Either the transmission sound is only laid on one track, or the same sound is laid on both.

Stereo	There are two types:
	
	Left and Right ('A and B')
	Generally recorded with two microphones very close together pointing in different directions.
	    A mono feed can be made by adding A and B together.
	
	Middle and Side ('M and S')
	The Middle signal covers most of the sound field. The Side signal carries enough information to generate a stereo image, but isn't actually a stereo signal. Added to the 'M' signal it gives 'A', and when subtracted from the 'M' signal it gives 'B'.
	    The 'M' signal is also the mono signal.

Split Tracks	Used extensively in news, where the journalist's voice is laid on one track, interviews and natural sound on the other. The tracks are either 'mixed down' before transmission and re-laid on tape, or left separate and the studio sound mixer puts both tracks on air.

Standard video tape audio formats

Briefing sound

There is no point in having pictures on air if you don't have the right sound to go with them. This can only be achieved by giving the sound department adequate information in sufficient time. While different broadcasters and countries run slightly different systems, generally sound departments have the same questions.

Before the programme reaches the studio

- How many people are involved in the programme? Are they moving or static (i.e. do they need radio or cabled microphones)?
- What are the presenters' talkback requirements (radio or cabled, open or switched)?
- Are there any specialist sound recording techniques (underwater/noisy props etc.)?
- What music or sound effects (spot effects) are required?
- Are there going to be outside sources or phone interviews?
- Most regular programmes have a standard rig (that goes for cameras as well as sound). Generally sound want to know what is *different* from normal.

When you get to the studio

- They want an accurate script or running order, which clearly shows where the spot effects or music are to be played.
- They want a seating plan showing who will be sitting where.
- They will need enough time to set levels from each of your contributors, and to line up all the incoming sources (VT, OS, etc.).
- Ideally they like to hear the beginnings and ends of all inserts.

Courtesy New Delhi Television

Many sound control rooms (SCR) work a two-person operation. While one concentrates on mixing the programme, the other checks and lines up incoming sources (outside broadcasts via satellite, microwave, VSAT etc.).

Sound commands

Both cameras and sound have a standard shorthand, although the traditional sound commands are beginning to be a bit dated.

Use the word 'Go' for cueing sound effects. Do not use 'go' for any other group of operators. 'Fade up/fade down/lose sound' are also permitted.

Who is doing what, where and when?

Tell sound what is happening next (this also applies to cameras, vision mixers etc.).

If you are cutting to a machine next (VT, Laser disk, Telecine etc.) be clear which one (many news studios have six VT machines).

Be clear if there should be more than one sound source live simultaneously, 'Coming to underlay VT D, John to voice over, titles music continues from VT A'.

Voice overs (underlays)

This is one area where there does not yet seem to be an international standard description. In the diagram opposite you can see some of the different ways people say the same thing. In each case the presenter will voice-over some video tape pictures.

I use the expression 'Underlay', shortened in written form to **ULAY**. The reason to choose this over VO is purely practical – if you're sitting in front of a large bank of monitors with video tape clocks, it is easier to differentiate the words VT and ULAY then VT and VO.

You must be clear whether you are running an underlay or a VT. Sound kill mics that are not being used to prevent background noise from going to air. If you are not clear that a tape is an underlay, you are likely to lose the presenter's voice.

Large interviews

During interviews with many participants, if you know that certain guests are not involved, then sound can fade, or 'take out' their microphones, reducing the amount of background noise.

Discipline your presenters

Do not let presenters say anything libellous or crude when they are wearing a mic. Too many careers have been terminated by somebody saying something stupid on the rare occasion sound have left the mic live, and it has gone straight to air. This is a 'no-brainer' – you have nothing to gain and everything to lose.

FX	effects
Grams	sound effects from gramophone (the old word for vinyl record player)
Mic	microphone
VO	Voice Over
SOT	Sound On Tape
UPSOT	Up Sound On Tape
SOVT	Sound on Video Tape

OOV	Out Of Vision
UNDER	Underlay
ULAY	**Underlay**
OLAY	Overlay
VO	Voice Over
LVO	Live Voice Over

Note: These all mean the same thing

Sound commands

We always used to say what machine was being used, i.e. 'Go tape', or 'Go grams'. However, sound departments have ruthlessly cashed in on technology and now use a huge range of sources (CD players, carts, floppy disks, hard disk systems, grams, DT, ¼ inch tape etc.). It is now accepted practice for directors to standby the sound required instead of the machine.

'Standby opening sting ... and go sting.'

Director's audio monitoring

Your sound equipment

The director usually has a range of sound monitoring equipment built into the desk. Please learn how to use it. It has been painstakingly built for your benefit.

Set the programme sound level so that you can comfortably hear it without it drowning everything and everybody else.

Set the incoming talkback level from your floor manager to a comfortable level.

Your talkback microphone needs to be switched on (many have a mute switch with a red warning light when the mic is cut off).

If you have outside broadcasts coming in to your programme, check and set your talkback levels to them.

Pre-hears

These are selectable sources, and may be outside sources (e.g. an outside broadcast unit) or a single person (e.g. your presenter). Depending on the complexity of your programme you may need to hear different sources at different times. Try to keep the number of pre-hears to a minimum – it makes a noise for everyone else, and if you have too many open at a time then you end up not being able to distinguish any.

Cut and dim switches

Occasionally it is acceptable to reduce the programme volume. Typically this would be during a long VT, once you know it is on air and sounds fine. If you have a number of programme running order changes to announce it makes sense to reduce the background noise.

If you have a dim/cut switch, use that to reduce the sound to a pre-set level. When you have finished, flick the switch back to normal and the volume returns to the old level.

Cue tracks

Some broadcasters transmitting in mono use the second track to lay cue pips, which can be heard in the control rooms. Typically a pip is recorded 10 seconds before the end of each insert, and another at the end. This deceptively simple system makes it very easy for everyone to know when a tape is about to end, and reduces dependency on accurate timings. It sounds neanderthal, but it works. If you are using this system, check your monitoring level.

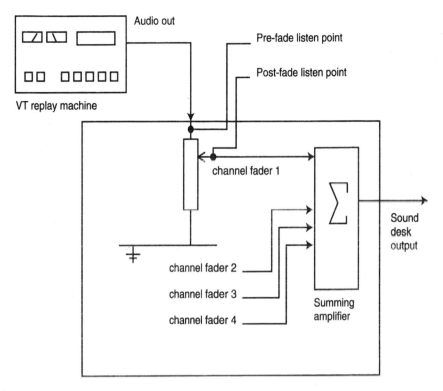

Simplified 4 channel sound desk

Pre-fade listen

This is the source at the sound desk before it has been faded up.

It differs from listening to the audio out of the VT as it tells you what is actually arriving at the sound desk, not what the VT is sending.

Asking for a pre-fade listen means you want to hear a source without the sound going to air, e.g. if you want to check the top of a tape, or need to hear what a guest is saying.

Post-fade listen

This is the source once it has passed through the channel fader.

You will only be able to hear this source if the fader is open and is part of the sound desk output.

83

Lighting and vision control

This is where the technical operators try to get the best looking pictures out of your cameras.

Monitoring
Without good quality monitoring it is impossible to get good pictures. Unless the technicians can really see the colours, brightness and contrast as it will be recorded they cannot make the necessary adjustments.

Matching cameras
One of the main aims of vision control is to prevent jumps in exposure and colour when you cut between cameras. This is harder to achieve than it sounds.

Lighting control
You will often have a lighting panel operator as well as a lighting director. On big sets where many adjustments to lighting levels are made, the lighting director and panel operator will have their own talkback circuit so that they can make the changes without disturbing everyone else.

Camera exposure
The cameras have two main exposure controls: gain (contrast) and lift (brightness).

Lift controls the black level. If it is too low, or 'crushed', the picture loses all detail in the darker areas. If it is set too high, the parts that should be black will come out as grey.

Gain controls the aperture of the iris (a device in the lens that controls the amount of light let through). If you open the aperture too much then the picture will 'burn out', in other words you lose skin colour and detail, ending up with large solid white patches everywhere.

Colour balancing
While we all understand getting the colours right in the bright part of a picture, many people do not realise that you have to match the colours in the dark parts as well. The classic example is shooting a police drama. If the dark parts of the picture do not have perfectly matched colours, the uniforms jump from black to dark blue, to a rather fetching brownish sort of colour.

Generally lighting need to be left to get on with their job during rehearsals. There is no point in telling them there is something wrong if they are still setting their lights. On the flip side, do brief them clearly beforehand if there is a particular effect you want.

Original still. This has a reasonable contrast range – the blacks are dark without losing detail (look at the texture in her coat).

The whites are bright without being burnt out (we have full detail in her face).

The gradation on the right-hand side shows a full range of black and white.

The same still once it has been 'crushed'. The blacks are far too dark, and we've lost most of the detail in her coat. She is approaching the point where she will look like a floating head.

The whites are bright and we have the full range from black to white, so this is not the same as underexposure.

'Lifting' and image has the opposite effect. Now none of the blacks are terribly dark, but the whites are still at the right level.

The gradation show the truncated contrast range that only goes from grey to white.

This is not the same as overexposure, a common mistake by many directors.

The effects of altering 'lift' on a television picture

85

Colour and light

Coloured light is additive

If you take a beam of white light and pass it through a prism it splits up into its component parts (red, orange, yellow, green, blue, indigo and violet). If you take all those coloured lights and mix them together you would end up with white light again.

For television we use a good approximation to those seven colours, red, green and blue. White equals all three, black equals none of them, and most other colours can be made up by mixing different amounts of these three coloured lights together.

This is the opposite of painting, which has red, yellow and blue as the primary colours (or more accurately magenta, yellow and cyan). Paint subtracts light, i.e. it prevents colours from being reflected.

Quantity

To put not too fine a point on it, outside is bright, inside is dark. The human eye can cope with a huge range in brightness, but even it sometimes takes a few seconds to get used to how dark a room is when you walk in from bright sunlight.

Colour

The human eye also sorts out one of the other problems with light – the fact that it keeps changing colour. From morning, through noon, to dusk the colour of what we think of as 'white light' changes. While the human eye makes natural adjustments, a camera doesn't and needs to be regularly calibrated to produce white-coloured whites.

Where we notice this most is when we shoot using tungsten (ordinary) lights instead of sunlight. Pictures will come out very yellow if we don't set the camera correctly or use filters to adjust for the difference. 'White balancing' is usually done by holding a piece of white card in front of the camera and pressing an auto balance button.

Colour temperature

You will hear lights being referred to by their 'colour temperature', which helps the camera operators set their filtering for balanced whites.

If you heat a piece of metal it start to glow red. Keep heating it, and by the time it is at 3200 Kelvin (K) it glows bright yellow (the same colour light as a normal light bulb). If you were able to heat it to 5600 K it would be glowing the same colour as daylight.

The original still again, restored to its correct contrast range.

The image underexposed (not enough 'gain', or the iris is too closed). We still have some detail in the blacks, and they are fairly dark so we know they have been correctly set.

The white parts of the picture ... aren't. The whitest this picture gets is grey (visible on the gradation band).

This is overexposing the picture. Again the blacks are pretty good – detail is visible and they are solid and dark.

The whites are 'burning out', i.e. we are losing detail in the brightest areas of the picture. This is particularly important on faces, and in this example we have lost all the character in her face.

Reducing the iris setting (pulling the 'gain' down) will correct the problem.

The effects of altering 'gain' on a television picture

Three point lighting

All classic lighting texts talk about three point lighting. As directors we must understand what the lighting director is trying to achieve, and be able to talk in a sensible language about any problems we have with the lighting. There is no point in just saying 'The lighting looks dreadful' without being able to say what it is that bothers you.

The key light
This is the strongest and hardest light, and provides deliberate shadows on a face. It gives 'modelling' to a person, and gets away from flat, lifeless pictures. The key light is typically placed 45° off the camera axis, and at a 30–45° downward angle.

Lighting designers will usually try to make this light naturally motivated. Often key lights come through set windows to simulate daylight.

The fill
Key lights give a very high contrast between the lit and shadowed parts of a face, and if we don't control and balance this contrast range the shadows will come out as black patches. This balancing is usually done with a large 'soft' light placed on the opposite side of the camera, near the camera axis. Most lighting directors will try to avoid unnatural multiple shadows.

Typically the soft light will be half the brightness of the key light, depending on the mood the lighting director is trying to create.

The backlight
This is usually a fairly hard light set behind the performer to light the top of the head and shoulders. It provides separation from the background (which is why it's sometimes known as a separation light). The trick with backlights is to add sparkle to hair without it being too obvious.

The background light
OK, I know we all talk about three point lighting, but we usually have to light the background behind our subject as well. This light is used to provide a sensible balance between the foreground and background.

Multiple subjects
Most lighting directors will be trying to give key, fill and backlights to all subjects, and may use one light for two functions. So, for example, if an interview is taking place the key light for the interviewer may double up as the backlight for the guest.

Backlight

Background light

Fill

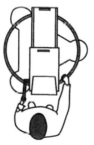

Key

Studio lighting

Rigging and lighting a set is a time-consuming affair, so it is vital the lighting director gets a clear brief before he begins his work.

Rigging
The time it takes to rig lights will depend on the size and complexity of the set, and the equipment the lighting director is working with. Ideally the lighting rig should have great height, be fully motorised (so that each light can be brought down separately) and be a saturation rig (so that lights can be placed anywhere).

This isn't necessary for all programmes. If you are using a permanent set you don't need the flexibility to remove all your lights quickly, so motorising the rig may be unnecessary. Many news and current affairs programmes use relatively low ceilings with fixed lights. These reduced studio heights can substantially reduce building rental costs.

Lighting during rehearsals
In the ideal world the lighting department is given enough time to rig and set lights so that when you are rehearsing your programme there is little interference. Tighter budgets make it impractical to take a studio out of service for a full day to set lights for anything but the largest productions. Lighting directors now work around performers during rehearsals.

While this may be an inconvenience there is precious little you can do about it. Most lighting crews have their own radio talkback circuit, to communicate with the lighting and vision control room without going across production talkback.

Fluorescent lighting
There are a few reasons why some studios choose to use fluorescent lighting over normal (tungsten) lights. In some buildings air-conditioning is inadequate for the heat of conventional lights. Fluorescent lights burn cold, so air-conditioning requirements are greatly reduced.

Electricity supplies are unreliable in some cities, and the lower power consumption of fluorescent lights means they can be run off generators and batteries more easily.

Where lights hang sufficiently low that people can touch them, tungsten lights, which get dangerously hot, can cause severe burns. Fluorescent lights are cold to the touch.

The soft lights are fine, but it is difficult as yet to get any serious modelling out of the harder fluorescent lights. Some people successfully mix the two forms of lights – fluorescents for the softs with a few tungstens for key lights.

Comprehensive lighting rigs give studios the ability to change quickly between different sets. The height also allows lights not being used to be kept clear.

91

VT (1)

Whether VT replay is from separate (stand alone) machines, from a cart or off non-linear replay, the directing skills remain similar.

The single most important fact

Most television studios have thousands of tapes. Some have hundreds of thousands. If you lose a tape that is not properly labelled you could spend years looking for it.

VT clocks

If you are sitting in front of a bank of monitors directing a live programme you want to know beyond a shadow of doubt that the tape you are about to roll is the right one.

The one simple proven method is to have a clock on the front of the tape saying what it is. The diagram opposite shows an example, with a title, and transmission date. There may be other information, including which edit suite was used to cut it – a useful reference if you find a technical problem with the tape.

Some places do not use clocks, but park the VT on the first frame. While it may be possible to identify the story from that frame, obviously there will be many occasions when you can't, in which case the director has to rely completely on the VT operator. VT operators have been known to make mistakes when they are busy.

Instant starts

Most people are using instant starts (i.e. the moment you roll a tape you can cut to it). While this has made the director's job easier, sequences now involve more tapes and complicated effects.

Pre-rolls

If you are working in a studio that does not have instant starts then you need to roll the tapes either 3 or 5 seconds before they go to air depending on the type of machine you are using, and the local standard. This is using a pre-roll.

Most people speak three words a second, although that does vary in some languages. If you are using a 5 second pre-roll, count 15 words back from the point you want the VT to appear. **Mark this point clearly on your script**, and when your presenter reaches it, roll the tape.

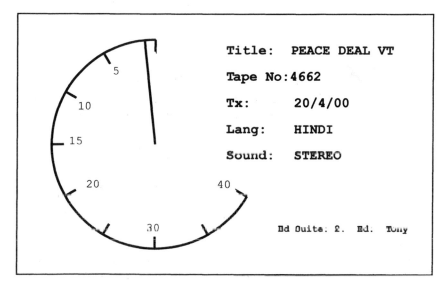

Title: PEACE DEAL VT

Tape No:4662

Tx: 20/4/00

Lang: HINDI

Sound: STEREO

Ed Suite: 2. Ed. Tony

A typical VT clock

The clock title must match the story title on the script.

Always use black and white letters only – some colours which look very pretty (e.g. dark blue) are illegible on a black and white monitor.

Never use flashing text. Murphy's law states the tape will always be lined up to where the flash was 'off', leaving the director with a blank clock.

Some information in a small font is acceptable – the edit suite and editor is a useful reference in case you find technical problems with the VT.

Different companies will require different information – e.g. some insist on the tape duration being displayed.

VT (2)

Protection copies
Some tapes are used day in, day out. Typically these are titles, break stings, graphics backgrounds etc. It is worth having a second copy of these tapes standing by in case your set gets chewed up or a bit worn out.

Assigning machines
Some studios run with a system of the director deciding before the programme begins which machine will be used to replay each tape. You can mark up your script in advance, but it can cause confusion if there are many changes to the running order, with two tapes being needed back to back from the same machine. Obviously you would need to re-assign during the programme.

Other people assign machines as they go along, leaving most of the decisions to the VT operator. This is the system I prefer as a good VT operator will make intelligent decisions and work around any machine problems without you even knowing about them.

Cart machines
These became popular with programmes that use many tape inserts. News, sport and magazine shows often go through dozens of tapes. One of the breakfast television shows in Britain rolls approximately 180 tapes each morning, so it makes sense to have a computer helping out.

Carts are a stack of separate machines that are automatically loaded with tapes in the right order. Remotely run, usually by the PA or director, you give exactly the same instructions for a cart as for stand alone machines.

Non-linear systems
Some broadcasters copy the edited tape into a non-linear playout device. Others are beginning to edit directly onto the non-linear machine, bypassing edited videotape altogether.

From the director's point of view there is very little difference between a cart machine and a non-linear player. The stories need to be offered up in the right order and the instructions to the technical staff remain the same. Non-linear playout devices are much faster at loading up new stories, but the internal 'housekeeping' of the video storage can be a nightmare, with someone having to archive off stories you no longer need.

Time-code
This is the signal recorded onto the VT to identify individual frames. Some studios use a device to superimpose the time-code onto the VT picture in the monitor stack.

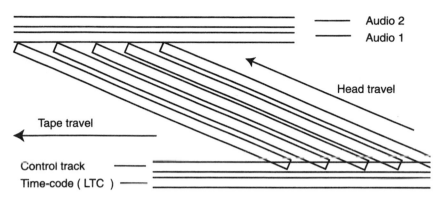

Audio 2
Audio 1

Head travel

Tape travel

Control track
Time-code (LTC)

Simplified track layout (Beta SP)

A time-code reader display

Set to display hours/mins/secs only, superimposed over a VT picture in a monitor stack.

Pros:
You can tell the VT operator exactly how far back or forward you want him to move the tape.

If you have many capgens to add, getting the time-code points gives you an absolute reference that is visible to everyone.

Cons:
You can't see a small part of the picture.

95

Prompters

Often ignored by directors, this operation is vital to the smooth running of a programme. If the wrong story is on the prompter, either the presenter will read it, leaving you in trouble, or read off their hard copy, leaving you shooting the top of their head.

Directors and prompters

The most important information a prompter needs is what is the next story? Also, if a story has been re-written, does it need to be downloaded into the prompting device?

In some studios presenters talk directly to prompters to change script words. Be aware that your prompter may be busy typing in information for the presenter.

You will often have a prompter monitor in the production control room. This is very useful, although many directors fail to make full use of it. Check it before each story to make sure it has the correct story ready for your presenter.

If you get horribly lost and completely lose track of the script your presenter is reading, then follow through on the prompter monitor. When they get to the end, roll your VT (it really is as simple as that, but only if you're using instant start VTs!).

If you see your prompting monitor go blank either your monitor or the prompting system has failed. Warn the presenter to have their hard copy ready while you work out which has happened. All presenters should keep an up-to-date script in front of them in case of problems, but some rely on the prompter too much.

Colour changes with prompters

A studio camera normally needs to be colour balanced once a prompter has been mounted – i.e. light from the prompter unit will cause your camera picture to shift colour slightly.

Hand-held cameras

Small, lightweight flatscreen liquid crystal displays (LCD) can be used on hand-held cameras, although they are easy to damage and the small display is limiting, but if the cameras are working close to your presenters they are still a huge help.

Prompters using TFT screen technology are lighter than their predecessors, and can be used indoors or outdoors.

For studio use the flatter design interferes less with the camera's ability to tilt (some of the older prompting monitors hit the pedestal ring if the camera was tilted down too far).

97

One plus one

Interviews are bread and butter work to directors, and are often conducted live. Once you can do simple interviews with few cameras it is easy to tackle larger set-ups.

Interview styles

First work out what style of interview you want. If we place the interviewer and the interviewee directly across a table from each other, it appears to be confrontational. If we place them near each other with a coffee table between them it becomes a much softer environment.

Two-eyed shots

I know it sounds completely self-explanatory, but some people still don't get it. A two-eyed shot is where we can see both of the eyes of a person. I cannot over-stress the importance of seeing the eyes. If we speak to someone we look directly into their eyes. If they won't look at us when they're speaking, we think they're shifty.

If you shoot someone from the side on (a profile shot), we can't see what their eyes are saying. We can see their nose. All of it. Anyone with a less than perfect hooter will not thank you for shooting them from the side.

Cross shooting

The obvious way to get two-eyed shots is to cross shoot. So, in the diagram opposite, Camera 1 gets the guest, Camera 3 picks up the interviewer and Camera 2 can float around from side to side.

Camera positioning

While it might seem obvious to lay out the cameras from left to right, 1 to 3, there is something to be said for reversing this order. If you look at the monitor stack, you would get a more natural view of the interview by reversing the cameras.

Camera shots

You can easily shoot a professional-looking one plus one interview programme with two cameras. It's less work with three, but if you can do it with two you'll find it easier to cope with larger groups.

The two main shots you will use are from the sides, MCU or MS, depending on the programme style. Additionally these cameras can offer 2-shots, or OTS. If you have a third camera in the middle it can move to one of the sides to offer a 2-shot at the same time as the single from a side camera, or it can offer a wider geography shot from nearer the middle.

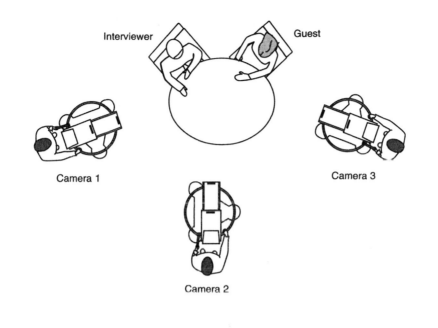

Interviewer

Guest

Camera 1

Camera 3

Camera 2

Camera 1

Camera 2

Camera 3

99

The classic clean interview

Ignoring the very beginning and end of the programme, which we'll cover later, the central part of an interview needs certain shots at specific times.
During the introduction of the guest we need to see them. Obvious, but a point missed by numerous people. Have the shot of the guest ready for when the interviewer introduces them. Immediately after the interviewer says 'Joining me in the studio is …' we should see the guest shot cut to air.
Near the top of the programme it is good practice to get a geography shot in. This sets up the stage, and shows the audience where the two people are in relation to each other. We will usually caption a person near the top of the programme. Additionally it is quite acceptable to caption them again later in the programme, particularly if they are not well known.
The exception is often the leader or prime minister of a country. It's a reasonable assumption that the vast majority of Americans know who their President is, so if you are making a programme for US consumption, why caption him?

Reaction shots
There is a great temptation when directing interviews to always use a shot of the person speaking. This can be visually dull, and is completely unnecessary, as the audience knows who is talking and can hear what they are saying even if they can't see them. Much better is to add to the programme by picking up reactions from other people involved in the interview. If, for example, a guest disagrees strongly with a point of view, the audience will only know that if you show them his reaction (e.g. shaking head).
Reaction shots don't have to be very long, but please make them long enough that they don't look like a mistake.

Getting from 2-shot to 2-shot
Some people don't like cutting from a 2-shot on one side to the 2-shot on the other side. If you fall in that camp and you are only using two cameras, you'll have to get used to the following sequence: 2-shot favouring interviewer, single guest, single interviewer (reaction shot), 2-shot favouring guest. Clearly the same sequence works the other way around.

Zooming in during an interview
Having said that reaction shots improve an interview, there are times when you shouldn't keep changing shot. If the guest is utterly captivating, then don't interfere and distract from them – just leave the shot as it is.
Slowly zooming in can also be highly effective, particularly as the interview develops to its climax. This may be an emotional description of an event, it may be finally getting the truth from a politician. Finishing on a close up or big close up with a few seconds silence can be very powerful particularly if the interviewer doesn't leap in and break the moment.

```
VT                              OPENING TITLES
Opening Titles


1_____/
MCU JOHN                        JOHN
                                Hello, and welcome to
                                'Spotlight'.  As juvenile crime
                                rates climb ever upwards, we
                                ask, what can be done to stop
                                the rot?


3_____Joining me in the  studio is/
MCU Doctor                      Dr DRAG-E-CHE-VICH, a
                                specialist in youth behaviour,
                                and author  of `Young crime:
2_____an old problem'./
2-Shot fav John
                                Dr DRAG-E-CHE-VICH, you don't
                                believe this is a modern
3_____phenomenon?/
A/B
                                DR DRAGICEVICH REPLIES
Capgen: Dr Dragicevich
Youth Behaviour Specialist
1_____/
A/B
                                JOHN
                                We all know the problem.  But
3_____what are the solutions? /
A/B
                                DR DRAGICEVICH REPLIES
```

Typical simple interview script with basic camera shots

One plus two (1)

The 'one interviewer, two guest' scenario has the same basic rules as the one plus one, but with a couple of variations. The interviewer can either be put between the guests, or to one side.

Interviewer to one side
This is the easier arrangement to shoot, particularly if you have only two cameras.

Two cameras
The interviewer has his own camera (Cam 1). This can get either a single (MCU or MS) of the interviewer, or it can crab slightly around to the right and get a 3-shot.

Camera 2 gets the single of either guest, a 2-shot of 'A' and 'B', or a 3-shot.

In this situation you need to throw in a lot of reaction shots from camera 1 while camera 2 reframes.

Three cameras
Now it becomes straightforward.

The interviewer works to camera (Cam 1). This gets either a single (MCU or MS), or crabs to the right to get a 3-shot.

Camera 2 gets either a single of guest 'A', a 2-shot of 'A' and 'B', or a 3-shot.

Camera 3 can get a single of either guest, or a 2-shot of 'A' and 'B'.

Generally we would have camera 2 pick up the single of the guest in the middle, while camera 3 picks up guest 'B'. This gives good two-eyed shots on both guests at the same time.

This arrangement works particularly well if the guests are friendly to each other. You can get nice 2-shots of guest 'B' listening to guest 'A', which is useful in a relaxed chat show, where you might want to see someone laughing at a story being told. It can work between politicians, but only if they are polite. With your interviewer trapped at one end of the desk it is very hard for them to jump in and take control if the guests become too obstreperous.

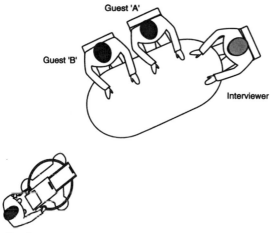

Guest 'A'

Guest 'B'

Interviewer

Cam 2

Cam 1

One plus two, two cameras

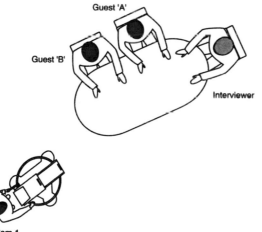

Guest 'A'

Guest 'B'

Interviewer

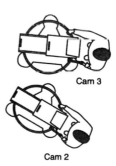

Cam 3

Cam 1

Cam 2

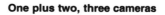

One plus two, three cameras

One plus two (2)

The second arrangement – of the interviewer in the middle – gives greater control to the interviewer, but is considerably harder to shoot.

Two cameras

It is virtually impossible to shoot well with just two cameras, but can be pulled off if you have a very capable interviewer who doesn't mind working to different cameras throughout the programme.

You have to position the cameras one on each side. With just a slight movement camera 1 can get a single of 'B', a 2-shot of interviewer and 'B' favouring 'B', a single of the interviewer talking to 'A', an OTS of 'A' favouring the interviewer, or a 3-shot.

Camera 2 gets the exact opposite.

The trick here is to get the interviewer to let you know who he will speak to next, either through some pre-arranged signal, or by the interviewer following the programme editor who calls out who will speak next.

Supposing you are on 'A' (Cam 2, MCU). If you know the interviewer will speak to 'A' again next, call for either an MCU of the interviewer or an OTS on Cam 1.

However if you know that 'B' will be questioned next, then Cam 1 needs to offer the 3-shot or 2-shot right. As soon as you cut 1, Cam 2 must offer the MCU of the interviewer looking at 'B'. Cut to Cam 2 as soon as it is ready, letting Cam 1 reframe on an MCU of 'B'.

It may sound a little daunting, but you get used to sequences like this once you have run them a couple of times.

Three cameras

You still have two cameras off to the sides (but now they are 1 and 3) which offer the same shots as above. Additionally, you can now risk crabbing either Cam 1 or Cam 3 further around to give an OTS of one guest looking straight at the other. This is a great shot if they start going directly at each other.

Cam 2 would normally start in the middle, where it would be the interviewer's main camera. This can crab left and right, but its most useful place for the bulk of the interview is probably hard round to one side, where it can offer a 2-shot left favouring 'A', a 2-shot right favouring the interviewer, or a 3-shot. Cam 3 gets either an MCU or an OTS of 'A'.

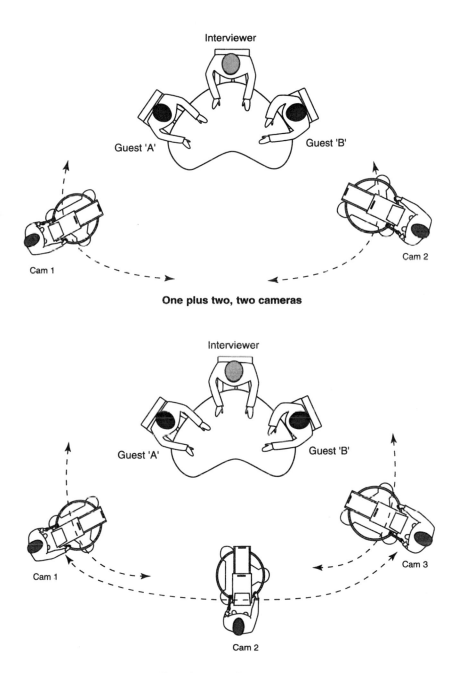

Interviewer

Guest 'A'

Guest 'B'

Cam 1

Cam 2

One plus two, two cameras

Interviewer

Guest 'A'

Guest 'B'

Cam 1

Cam 2

Cam 3

One plus two, three cameras

105

Two plus two

This is a common format for early morning and daytime programmes, and is usually based around an inverted 'L' shaped set. While it is possible to shoot with three cameras, to have total flexibility you really need four.

Camera shots

In the diagram shown, cameras 3 and 4 concentrate on the presenters. If you need both on shot at the same time then camera 4 shoots presenter 2 and camera 3 gets presenter 1. This gives reasonable eyelines to both presenters.

If you know for certain which presenter will be speaking next then shoot them on camera 4, which will always get the better eyeline. Camera 3 can then crab slightly to the left to offer a wide shot as a 'get out clause' if the other presenter speaks.

Cameras 1 and 2 play similar roles with the guests. If you need both at the same time, then camera 1 shoots guest 'B' and camera 2 shoots guest 'A'; otherwise shoot the guest that is speaking on camera 1 and get camera 2 to offer a 2-shot.

Two plus three

This type of set-up easily extends if you need to bring in an extra guest. Many programmes design the seating so that a 'jump seat' can be added to the guests' end of the sofa.

The roles of the cameras don't change greatly, except that you will generally be better off having camera 2 offer a group shot, with camera 1 always getting the single shots of the guests.

Controlling the interview

The difficulty in a two plus two interview is the co-ordination between the presenters. Most presenting teams develop a silent method of communication so that they don't both ask questions at the same time.

The end of an interview

You know that at the end of an interview your presenter will thank the guests. Have a shot of them ready – it should never catch a director by surprise. Make sure your presenter knows which camera to work to next.

'Last answer. John thank the guests, then Jenny, story 4, camera 4.'

Keep the guests sitting still

Many interviewees have a desire to run out of the studio the moment an interview is over, usually by walking in front of the camera in use and forgetting they're plugged into microphone cables. They must be briefed beforehand to stay seated until the floor manager moves them.

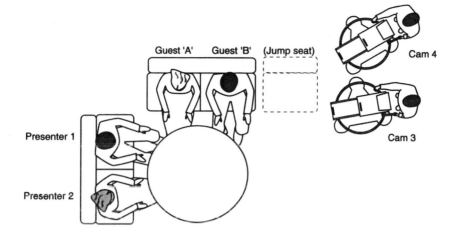

Guest 'A'   Guest 'B'   (Jump seat)   Cam 4

Cam 3

Presenter 1

Presenter 2

Cam 1

Cam 2

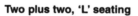

Two plus two, 'L' seating

One plus three

The 'round table' or 'square dance' interview is probably the hardest for new directors to tackle. The difficulty is 'the line' keeps moving, depending on who is talking to whom.

The line
As you can see, there are six 'lines'. This, for the benefit of those unencumbered with natural understanding of shooting interviews, should be enough to put off all but the hardiest. In theory we should only use the cameras on the same side of a line.

Typical shooting pattern
Suppose the presenter talks to guest 'A'. Camera 2 gets a single of the presenter or 2-shot favouring him. Camera 4 offers the same shots of guest 'A'. Even though it is technically 'crossing the line', camera 1 offers listening shots of either guest 'B' or guest 'C', whichever is most likely to disagree with guest 'A'.

The presenter next turns to guest 'C'. Now camera 3 is the single shot of the presenter, camera 1 provides the single of the guest he is addressing, while camera 4 gives listening shots.

If Guest 'A' now starts talking directly to guest 'C' you have a choice. With two cameras on each side of the line, you can either shoot with cameras 1 and 4, or 2 and 3. The choice will depend on where the conversation was before this direct across-the-table confrontation began. If the presenter was talking to guest 'C', then you would use 2 and 3 (to keep guest 'C' still looking to the right-hand side of frame), but if guest 'C' had been talking to guest 'B' then it would be better to use cameras 1 and 4 (having just come off cameras 4 and 2).

Tricks
There is a neutral shot using a vertically mounted camera directly above the table, giving a view very similar to that in the diagram. Dead handy, you can cut to it at any time.

The cameras will have to move left and right to get clean singles and sensible OTS shots. Remember, we don't have to see the person speaking instantaneously – the audience can hear everything being said. Get to a wide shot first, work out the correct camera and then get to the close-up shot.

Wide shots
Usually you will have two cameras offering singles, one a listening shot, and the other is spare. Always make this camera offer a wide shot. If you are in trouble, cut to this, and work out the correct camera to use. Sitting on a wide shot for a while works just fine.

108

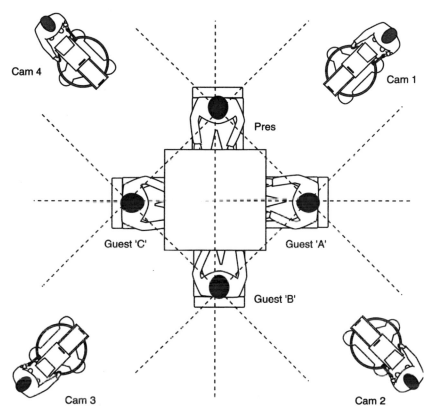

Cam 4

Cam 1

Pres

Guest 'C'

Guest 'A'

Guest 'B'

Cam 3

Cam 2

One plus three, square seating

109

Audience interview shows

Audience interview shows were made popular by the likes of Oprah Winfrey and Ricki Lake, and viewers who wanted to tell the whole world about their embarrassing pasts. They involve active participation from the audience, who are encouraged to stand up and throw questions forward.

There are obviously many different sets and formats, but there are two fundamental types of audience interview programmes.

Presenter stays in fixed position
This is the easier situation to shoot, and while there are many ways you can position your cameras, the example that follows (a 1+4+audience) is a useful starting point.

Crossing the line
OK, I admit it. In this type of programme you constantly cross the line. The trick here is to throw in 'neutral shots' to cover the jump.

Camera shots
You need quite a few cameras to shoot this well. I recommend a minimum of five, although six is a more useful starting point.

In the diagram cameras 1, 2 and 3 are in conventional interviewing positions, cross-shooting the presenter and his guests. The presenter works to camera 1, which would have a prompter unit.

Camera 4 has a big lens (i.e. a good range from wide to very narrow). It is positioned just above the back row of the audience, behind a backdrop. It can offer a wide shot showing the back of the audience, the presenter and guests and the stage backdrop behind them. It can also zoom in to a group shot, or further to an MCU of any guest.

Cameras 5 and 6 are positioned high and behind the presenter and guests. Normally camera 5 offers a reasonably wide shot of the audience, while camera 6 hunts for single shots.

Camera 7 is an audience camera which gives some nice shots of audience members, depending on where they are seated. It is able to get several members of the audience in the same shot without having to go too wide.

Cameras 4, 5 and 6 are all positioned pretty well straight down the middle line of the studio, so most of their shots are 'neutral', i.e. the eyelines of most people run straight up through the axis of the camera.

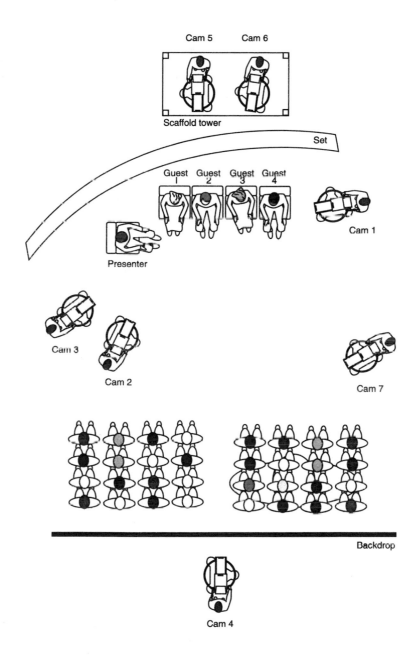

Cam 5   Cam 6

Scaffold tower

Set

Guest 1   Guest 2   Guest 3   Guest 4

Cam 1

Presenter

Cam 3

Cam 2

Cam 7

Backdrop

Cam 4

Shooting the programme

The start of the programme used as an example on the previous page will probably be like any ordinary interview programme, using cameras 1, 2 and 3, with 4 offering a group shot and 5 a reverse shot of the audience.

When the presenter asks for questions from the audience you can cut straight to camera 5 while 6 finds the single shot. While 6 hunts the single shot of the audience member talking, camera 4 would normally zoom to a single of the guest to whom the question is being asked.

Be aware that camera 6 has probably only got a tiny depth of field, as lighting on an audience is usually not too bright. You need either a very good camera operator, or to give them a reasonable amount of time finding the shot and focusing up.

Actions and reaction

The chances are the production team selected guests with differing opinions. Whenever one is speaking, at least one other will disagree. A good director will get plenty of strong reaction shots.

The cross-shooting cameras (2 and 3) can usually offer some great-looking shots of a guest talking to the audience with another guest disagreeing strongly.

Know the performers

You must know who is sitting where and their viewpoint. Then you can predict in advance who will clash with whom. Don't forget the audience will also have a viewpoint, so if a guest says something particularly provocative, try to get in some tight reaction shots of the studio audience.

Pre-prepared questions

Some programme formats use questions from the audience that have been prepared in advance. This has three advantages. You know you are going to get an intelligent question, you have time to get a good clean shot of them and you know where to point a microphone.

What you do need is a simple system of describing where the person will be sitting. Some studios break the seating area into different zones, rows and columns ('camera 6 next, lady, blue zone row 3, seat 6').

Sound

In many ways this is much harder than pictures. You will need multiple boom operators combined with personal microphones and ceiling slung mics. It takes a very experienced sound supervisor to mix those together and keep up the technical standard.

Ceiling-mounted cameras can provide useful cutaway shots during interviews. Mounted in cradles, they are either in a fixed position or fitted with remote control heads.

Shooting with mobile presenter

In this format the presenter is able to walk up to members of the audience, ask them about their experiences and invite them to direct questions to the programme guests.

Let's assume for this example that you have only four cameras, plus one slung overhead.

Camera positions

You have few options with limited resources. The best bet is two cameras at the front of the audience, who primarily work the audience and presenter, and two at the back who concentrate on the main guests.

A camera hung from the ceiling covering the audience and guests is useful as a source you can cut to at any time without fear of crossing the line or having someone block the shot.

Difficulties with limited cameras

If the presenter stands in the wrong place, or a member of the audience stands up it is possible that one of your cameras may be blocked out, leaving you with inadequate coverage. Under these circumstances it is helpful to have a presenter who is able to take instructions through an earpiece to move and clear the camera.

If the presenter or audience member stands directly in a line between a camera at the front and one at the back, both will have a camera in shot. In this case you need an alternative shot from either of your remaining cameras while the front camera crabs out of the way.

Shooting from the back

There are two main techniques for coverage of the guests by the back cameras. Either one camera offers a group shot of all guests while the second hunts single shots as directed, or they both work as single cameras.

In the first case the camera crew will quickly work out for themselves when they can change shots. In the second you have to call which camera you want to pick up which person every time.

Courtesy Anglia Television

The Time The Place is a daily live audience show. It uses two cameras hidden behind the audience (in dark roundels) and two cameras in front.

Half the programme is done with a guest or guests sitting at the front of the stage. During this part, all cameras are facing forward. Later the presenter walks into the studio audience to ask questions and let them put their views directly to the programme guest. At this time the front cameras swing around to cover the audience.

Clearly there is a danger of getting the front cameras in shot, and it is also easy for the presenter to stand right in front of one of the back cameras if he needs to speak to a member of the audience who is sitting in an inconvenient place.

The show uses five cameras, the fifth being mounted in the lighting rig.

Magazine shows

These programmes have a number of sections that may or may not be editorially connected. They use studios with a number of separate areas (often referred to by their function, e.g. interview area, demonstration area, kitchen etc.).

Large chunks of magazine shows may not have a full script, e.g. demonstrations, so running orders will simply have sections saying 'As directed'.

Clearing cameras
You will not have a complete set of cameras for each area. This is not a problem – camera pedestals have wheels. Feel free to use them.

It does mean you must be aware of when an item is about to finish, and 'clear' one or more cameras to the next area, ready to shoot the start of the following programme item.

The big danger in moving cameras around a studio to different areas is getting the camera pedestals caught in cable loops. Cables can be lifted over cameras, although that takes time. Cameras cannot run over cables.

Spinning cameras
Some magazine sets have two areas with the cameras in the middle. To shoot the second area, the cameras spin by 180°. Be aware that this effectively reverses the order of your cameras, and this will affect your view in the control room.

Switching directing styles
The nature of magazine programmes is that the directing technique changes depending on the item. One moment you may be directing a demonstration, where you decide which shots to use while the item is 'on air'. The next minute you may be running a very structured piece where you have a number of VTs and graphics which have to hit precise words on a script. There is a real difficulty of switching between the two styles at a moment's notice.

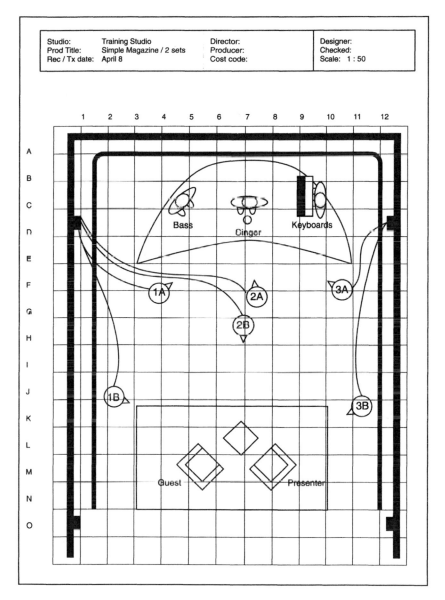

On a simple two-set magazine show like this the cameras would swing round to cover both areas. This changes the view in the control room (cameras left to right become right to left) but keeps the cables nice and neat.

Preparing demonstrations

Demonstrations cover anything from making toys on children's pro-grammes, to cooking, fashion parades etc.

Preparation is all

It is vital that you have done your homework as a director. You must know what the demonstration is all about, in what order events will take place, what the important or difficult bits are, and how your presenter is going to demonstrate it.

Find out well in advance what the demonstrator needs (electricity, water, fire etc.). Is the demonstration noisy? Is it dangerous? (A car in a studio can pump out carbon dioxide at a very unpleasant rate.)

Rehearsing

Find out if your demonstrator is left- or right-handed – it makes a great deal of difference as to which side you shoot your close-up shots from.

Have a clear structure for the demonstration, i.e. the order in which everything will happen, and make sure the presenter works to that.

Run through the action with a stopwatch before you even start looking at camera shots. Most demonstrations take much longer than people realise, and your presenter may need many rehearsals to complete the item in the allotted time. If it's too long, cut out sections rather than telling your pre-senter to go faster.

Bring lots of spare consumables. If you are going to destroy something during a rehearsal, make sure you have plenty of supplies to cover sever-al practice runs.

If the demonstration involves the presenter writing you need to decide at the rehearsal stage whether to place a camera behind them (to see from their viewpoint) or get them to hold up the finished item to a camera.

Keep small objects supported on a table. Most humans shake slightly. Most humans shake somewhat more when they have a camera pointing at them. Take that shaking, magnify it with a close-up shot of their hand and they can end up looking like a gibbering wreck.

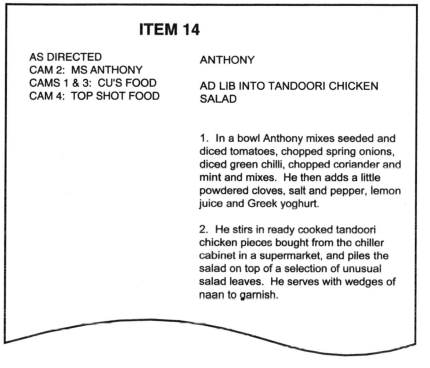

ITEM 14

AS DIRECTED
CAM 2: MS ANTHONY
CAMS 1 & 3: CU'S FOOD
CAM 4: TOP SHOT FOOD

ANTHONY

AD LIB INTO TANDOORI CHICKEN
SALAD

1. In a bowl Anthony mixes seeded and diced tomatoes, chopped spring onions, diced green chilli, chopped coriander and mint and mixes. He then adds a little powdered cloves, salt and pepper, lemon juice and Greek yoghurt.

2. He stirs in ready cooked tandoori chicken pieces bought from the chiller cabinet in a supermarket, and piles the salad on top of a selection of unusual salad leaves. He serves with wedges of naan to garnish.

© BBC

A typical script for a cookery programme

The director has declared the roles of the cameras, so the cook knows he always works to camera 2. There are two cameras picking up close-up shots of the food, and one camera mounted on the lighting rig looking down at the food.

The script shows the order in which the cooking will take place, and reminds the presenter of any points they need to mention (e.g. where to buy the ingredients). This also lets the director know when the cook is likely to be talking directly to camera.

Be aware that high mounted cameras can get steamed up if food is being heated underneath.

Shooting demonstrations

Give cameras a basic role, but be flexible.

Simple, basic coverage

There are two things you know you will need to see. Your presenter talking, and a close-up of what he is talking about. If you have these you have basic coverage. Obviously there are other shots you may want to have – wider shots, alternative close-up shots, top-down shots etc.

There are two main alternative presenter shots – a medium close-up (showing just their head and shoulders) or a mid shot, which shows the item in front of the presenter. Let your presenter know which is his camera, and where it will be.

As the demonstration progresses, let everyone know what will happen next. The camera crew would rather know that your presenter is about to put on a top hat, than hear you want lots of headroom without explaining why.

Close-up shots

Very few directors give too many close-up shots. We know what the item looks like. We've probably been seeing it all day in the studio, but the audience has not had that luxury.

Make sure you have close-up shots ready for when the demonstrator talks about an item. There is nothing worse than hearing about something and not being able to see it.

Let objects move out of frame on a close-up camera rather than try to follow. It is virtually impossible to follow any small object being lifted up and moved about. Let it go out of frame and cut to a wider shot.

Comparisons

The viewers don't know how big something is unless they have something to compare it with, so hands in shot give a useful scale.

If the demonstrator is comparing two objects, it is usually 'a good thing' to have both objects available in the same shot.

Animals and children

We can make presenters hold up inanimate objects in the right direction so that we can get nice clean shots. Animals and children aren't quite so predictable, so it is useful to have two cameras dedicated to close-up shots, and you simply call for whichever camera looks better when the item is being shot.

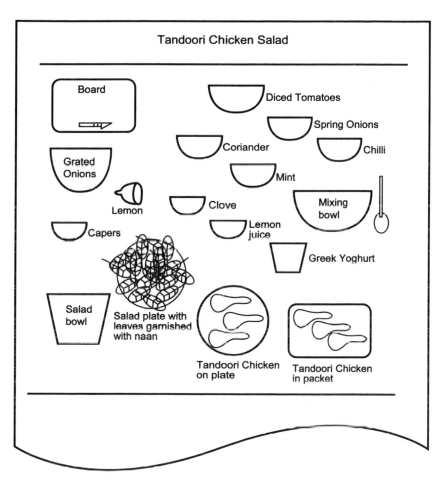

Tandoori Chicken Salad

Board

Diced Tomatoes

Spring Onions

Coriander

Chilli

Grated Onions

Mint

Lemon

Clove

Mixing bowl

Capers

Lemon juice

Greek Yoghurt

Salad bowl

Salad plate with leaves garnished with naan

Tandoori Chicken on plate

Tandoori Chicken in packet

Simple prop layouts are provided in scripts for demonstrations. They are also used by the props department and floor managers to make sure the ingredients are in the right place.

Follow the script through from the previous page to see how the ingredients are laid out in logical rows, without being as dull as one long straight line. This makes it easy for both the cook and the director.

Layout pictures like this do not have to be beautiful works of art, but they do have to show unambiguously the position of each item.

Music

This is a big subject with many variations and possibilities including pop, opera, classical etc., each of which uses different techniques. Some will require you to be shooting the musicians, others will have simultaneous stage actors.

However, there are some basics used in televising many genres of music.

Musical structure
Try to get hold of the basic breakdown of the song/music. For most western music this can be broken down into bars and words.

Coverage
Think about it like shooting a demonstration – what are the basic shots you need?

It is always worth having cover – the wide shot. At any stage during a performance you can cut to this and it will look adequate. At the beginning of a piece this lets the audience see everyone on the stage.

The lead singer (or soloist) justifies having a camera dedicated to them.

During the musical break it would obviously be useful to have shots of the solo instruments.

What are the main instruments during the opening sixteen bars?

At the end do you want to see applause from other people in the studio? Generally be very clear about how you intend to get into a musical number, and how you will get out again at the other end.

Scripts or score
Depending on the type of music and your ability to read a score, you may prefer to work off a marked-up music score.

Playback
Many studio performances are done over a backing tape. This simplifies the studio set-up greatly, but many performers are not terribly good at making it realistic.

Do not start on a tight shot of the first instrument for the first note.

It takes most musicians a second or two to sync up with the playback tape.

16 bar intro
Verse 1
Chorus
Verse 2
Chorus
16 bar musical break
Verse 3
Chorus
Chorus

Typical basic structure of a pop song. Most directors start by doing a basic breakdown of the song noting the singers and the key instruments for each part.

4 bars W/A Z/I to 2 shot singer and bass

2 bars drummer

6 bars CU keyboard Z/O and crab left to 3 shot

4 bars lead guitar

Each section is then broken down into the individual shots. This may include their time duration, but more commonly the number of bars the shot is to last.

Shot 1, 1 of 4, 2, 3, 4
2, 2, 3, 4
3, 2, 3, 4
4, 2, 3, 4

shot 2, 1 of 2, 2, 3, 4
2, 2, 3, 4

shot 3, 1 of 6, 2, 3, 4
2, 2, 3, 4
3, 2, 3, 4
4, 2, 3, 4
5, 2, 3, 4
6, 2, 3, 4

shot 4, 1 of 4, 2, 3, 4
2, 2, 3, 4
3, 2, 3, 4
4, 2, 3, 4

The production assistant's bar count. This can be ferociously fast, but it is very useful for both the vision mixer and the camera crews, who are able to judge how much time they have left to develop their shots.

Many of the camera cuts will have to be done just before the beat, otherwise you clip the beginning of someone singing or an instrument being played.

(Think of this as '1 and 2 and 3 and 4 CUT'.)

123

Standard script layouts

Technical operators receive new scripts every day from different production teams. If everyone uses the same standard layouts then they can extract the information they need quickly and efficiently.

Normal layout

There will be slight differences from company to company, but most people have a similar standard layout.

The page is divided into two main columns. The right-hand side has the script and stage instructions, along with sound effects.

The left-hand side has the shot number, the camera number and the shot description.

Timing of programmes

Most sit-com and drama producers know how many pages they need to fill their programme duration. It sounds a bit strange, just basing it on page numbers, but it seems to work in most cases.

This is dependent on the writers strictly adhering to the programme layout format. They cannot change the number of lines per page, the font size, the column widths or anything that will increase the number of letters they can fit on a line.

Cut lines

These are placed at the end of the word (or action) after which the cut is to take place. If you place it before the start of a word it doesn't give vision mixers long enough to react.

At the left-hand end of the cut line is the shot number. Above the line is the camera number (and sometimes the studio area being used). Below the line is a description of the shot.

Additional shots

During the rehearsal you may find you need extra shots. If you want one after shot 10, it is given the number 10A. When you create extra shots make sure you give clear information about it to the cameraman concerned, who will add it to his camera card.

```
(5 ON 1)                      PETER: (ON THE TELEPHONE)
                              You have a warm sexy voice on
                              the phone. (PAUSE, THEN HAPPY)
                              Nobody's ever said that to me
                              before.

6. 3_____        A KNOCK AT THE DOOR./
   WS Peter and door          PETER: (Contd., INTO PHONE)
                              There's someone here. Got to
7. 1_____        go./ Bye darling snocky
   MCU Peter                  pops.
8. 2_____/
   MLS Peter. Follow to door  PETER:(Contd.,WALKING TO DOOR)
                              Who is it?

                              SECURITY MAN:
9. 1_____        Security./
   A/B
                              PETER: (OPENING DOOR)
                              But I don't have any security
10. 3_____        here./
    Security man OTS Peter.
                              SECURITY MAN: (WALKING IN)
                              Tell me about it. I could
                              have been anybody. Without
                              24 hr Securecover you could
                              have had a complete stranger
                              in your house.

                              PETER:
                              I do have a complete stranger
11. 1_____        in my house./
    MCU Security Man
                              SECURITY MAN:(TURNS TO PETER)
                              Normally I have to work a
                              bit harder proving people
    © 1997                    need Securecover.
```

Example of standard script layout

Camera cards

These are the primary reference for the camera crew during rehearsals. They are also available during transmission as a reminder of their shots, which is why they are also known as crib cards.

Standard layout
Again it makes sense for everyone to lay out camera cards in the same way. The top of the page must contain the camera number and the programme name. Underneath that should be four columns, allowing for the shot number, the area of the set, the shot description and a space for the operator to make their own notes.

Accuracy
Information is transferred to the camera cards from the shooting script once the director has finished with it. It is absolutely vital that the cards are accurate. If shot descriptions are inaccurately copied over, you will receive the wrong shots.

If shot numbers are erroneous you will receive total mayhem.

Short and sweet
When a camera operator becomes busy they will not have time to read long complicated instructions, so shot descriptions are kept short and to standard abbreviations.

We also need to allow enough space on the cards for extra shots to be added during rehearsals.

As directed
Demonstrations and interviews obviously don't use pre-determined shot numbers, and a camera card for these types of 'As directed' sequences would simply state the primary role of each camera.

CAMERA   THREE   Title: THE SIT-COM CLASSIC   Ep. 3.

SHOT   POS   DESCRIPTION   NOTES

Sets: Living room / Hallway

SHOT	POS	DESCRIPTION	NOTES
1	A	MLS Peter vacuuming. Follow to magazine rack	
4	B	WS phone in f/g	
6	B	WS Peter and door	
10	B	Security man OTS Peter	

Typical camera card

127

VT scripts

Here we look at a simple single news story. It has an intro by the news-reader, followed by a VT.

VTR
This title (Anfield Video) matches the clock on the front of the VT and the name of this page of the script.

Tape number
The number should be written both on the tape itself and on its cover box.

IQ (in words)
Stands for 'In cue'. They are the first words on the tape, and are used by the VT operator to check they have the correct story lined up.

OQ (out words)
These are used by sound, the vision mixer and the director, who all specifically listen for the words written here. Normally the last two or three seconds of words on the VT are written here.

There are a couple of exceptions. If the VT finishes on music then you would just put 'Music out'. The other exception is when a programme has a standard way of finishing reports.

'John McKenzie at The Kop for the News at 8'.

This is known as a 'Standard out cue', shortened to SOQ, or a 'Sign-off'.

Duration
This must be accurate. The PA will use this information to count out of the VT.

Capgens
In this case the timings have been given with respect to the start of the report, i.e. the first capgen needs to appear 15 seconds into the report.

There are other ways of writing timings down, depending on the technical arrangements of your machines and the time-code formats used by the studio. For example, some studios have time-code readers from each VT machine. These numbers are superimposed on your VT monitors, and can be easily read by anyone in the control room. On the script the capgens would be written next to the time-code at which they are to appear.

(ANDY)

Liverpool Football Club
today launched their video
`The Last Night of the
Kop'. Proceeds from the
sale will go towards the
Barnardo's Merseyside
Centenary Appeal and
Liverpool FC Caring in the
Community.

It could be an significant
source of income, as John
McKenzie found out when he
went along to Barnado's.

VT: ANFIELD VIDEO

TAPE:21630

(VT)

IQ: `The players came out'

OQ: SOQ

Dur: 1.15

Capgens:

@ 0.15 The Kop, Liverpool

@ 0.30 Peter Levin,

    Barnado's

Example of VT script

News and current affairs

News programmes have the difficulty of very tight deadlines and stories that continue to change up to and during transmission. The main reference for most technical operators during a programme is a running order, although the director should always receive a full set of scripts.

Running order changes
If stories are not ready or live links not working there may be a change in the running order. When working off paper this means drawing arrows to show where stories have moved.

The director must clearly state any changes in running order. It is very easy for one person not to be aware of a change and you end up with the wrong graphic sitting behind the newsreader.

Once two or three stories have moved everyone's running order becomes very messy. In busy programmes like this it is even more important that the director clearly says what story is running next in sufficient time for everyone to respond.

This is where an electronic newsroom system is a great help. As a director you sit with a running order on a screen in front of you. As any move happens you see it instantly updated in front of you.

Killing stories
Most news producers like to start programmes with too much material rather than not enough. If they are planning a live link they should have enough stories to fill the bulletin if the link doesn't work. This means that some stories will have to be killed off during the programme. Again the director should very clearly say which stories have died.

Changing sources
Journalists will be editing right up to the start of, and sometimes during, the news bulletin. One way of getting these stories on air quicker is to have the edit suites available 'on-line'. That simply means the vision mixer and sound supervisor can cut to the edit suite directly.

Warn your crew if that is likely to happen as they will often have to dial up the appropriate edit suite on a matrix.

Story numbering
This used to be always sequential, with extra stories (if they are running after story 3; for example) being numbered 3A, 3B etc. Many organisations are switching over to non-sequential systems, so the director would say 'Story order now 3, 7, 9, 4'. Anyone with scripts will just move the stories to that order, without re-numbering them.

```
                              22.03.45 - 22.31.25  CB3.10
                              THURSDAY 23ᴿᴰ APRIL 1998 **ST1**
                              TREVOR McDONALD  Studio 1


PAGE  NC  TITLE/REPORTER        VTR   CAMERAS  GRAPHICS  (*standby)
=================================================================================

NEWS AT TEN TITLE  [TMcD] VTR    ! CT A  !              ! *BF: "NEWS AT TEN" [key left]
  CAMERA CRAB & TITLES RX VTR    ! ES    !4/Crab  !  FF: Newsroom C/K for MCU
00A   TM  BONGS  1 SUDAN         ! CT B  !        !  ! *FF: "NEWS AT TEN" Logo
               2 DUTROUX         ! CT C  !        !
               3 TICKETS         ! VT 37 !        !
               4 LINDA           ! VT 38 !        !
               5 SHEARER         ! CT B  !        !
                                 !       !        !
                                 !       !        !
10    TM  SUDAN/                 !       !1A/W    ! W:  "NEWS AT TEN" on black, CH >
10A       EWART VTR              ! CT A  !        ! W:  "FAMINE" STARVING PEOPLE
          (BACKUP ON VT 37)      !       !        ! FF: 888 key
                                 !       !        !
                                 !       !        !
20    TM  BACKREF                !       !1A/W    ! W:  "FAMINE" STARVING PEOPLE
                                 !       !        !
                                 !       !        !
30    TM  DUTROUX/               !       !1A/W    ! W:  "ESCAPE" DUTROUX
30A       NEELY VTR              ! CT B  !        !
                                 !       !        !
                                 !       !        !
40    TM  TICKETS/               !       !1A/W    ! W:  "FINES" TICKET / WORLD CUP
40A       MILLER SW VTR          ! CT C  !        !
                                 !       !        !
                                 !       !        !
50    TM  RAY                    !       !1A/W    ! W:  "EARL RAY" EARL RAY
                                 !       !        !
                                 !       !        !
60    TM  MP/                    !       !1A/W    ! W:  "EXPENSES" FIONA JONES / ROSE
60A       BRADBY VTR             ! VT 37 !        !
                                 !       !        !
                                 !       !        !
70A   TM  PRECOMS / LINDA        ! CT A  !2A/MCU  ! FF: Newsroom C/K for MCU
                     BOOKS       ! CT B  !        !
                     SHEARER     ! CT C  !        !
              /MUSIC STING/      !       !        ! CH: Precoms Sequence

---------------------------------------------------------------------------------

                  COMMERCIAL BREAK   3'10"

---------------------------------------------------------------------------------
```

Courtesy ITN

This is a paper running order as used by technical staff for a live evening news. The company decides ahead of transmission which VT machine will be used for each playout. If the tape isn't quite ready in time, any of the edit suites can be selected on the vision mixer and rolled straight to air.

If it is known in advance that a tape will be late or rolled from somewhere else down an outside source line, it will be marked as ES or OS on the script.

The complexity of the opening sequence is not untypical for a news programme.

131

As directed running order

Running orders for magazine shows break up into the separate segments, or sequences. The basic information that everyone wants to strip out of a running order like this is who is involved, where and when?

Timing

Magazine shows and non-scripted items are notorious for running over time. Most things take longer than we expect, and it is important that the PA keeps a firm grip on the programme timing throughout the show.

This running order shows both the expected duration of the item, and the time it should start. If the programme is running over an item will start late, and the PA can calculate how much time needs to be lost by subtracting the planned item time from the actual time.

Note that if an item is removed from the running order once it has been typed up, then all the time calculations from that point on will be wrong.

Camera roles

In the second column the director has worked out the basic functions of his cameras. These decisions will have been made on a number of criteria.

In this case cameras 1 and 4 only are fitted with prompter units, so the programme presenters (Melissa and Jenny) always present to one of those cameras.

Not all cameras may be mobile, particularly if you have steps as part of your set. While hand-held cameras may be the most flexible, they are also the most vulnerable to cables being pulled or caught. If you have a busy lightweight camera it is worth having a 'cable basher' to assist.

Overkill

You do not need five cameras to point at two people, so even if it is tempting to point everything at the main action, you may be better off having cameras ready in the next set, in case you need to drop out of an item early.

Also be aware how much space your cameras take. Full function studio cameras need large heavy pedestals. Three of those in a row use up a lot of your floor.

```
FRIDAY RUNAROUND       Running order: Friday Jan 16th 1998


TIME:        AREA/CAMS:          SEQ/ITEM/PAGE:        DUR:

15.00.00   STEPS                 SEQ 1/P1             1.00
           1:  2S                JENNY AND MELISSA
           2:  WS                HELLOS/LOOK AHEAD
           4:  MCU JENNY
_____

15.01.00      VT: TODAY'S HIGHLIGHTS                  0.30

_____

15.01.30   CAFÉ                  SEQ 2/P3             4.00
           3:  ANDREW            INTERVIEW ANDREW
           4:  MELISSA           SINGER/ANNOUNCE
           5:  2S                COMPETITION
_____

15.04.30      VT: SAD SONGS                           2.00

_____

15.06.30   CAVE                  SEQ 3/P6             4.00
           1:  JENNY             GUNK COMPETITION
           2:  3S                WITH TWO AUDIENCE
           5:  2S                MEMBERS
_____

15.10.30      VT: CARTOON MADNESS                     3.30
           (RESET CAVE FOR DANCE SEQ)
           (REH CLOSER)
_____
```

Magazine running order (as directed)

Electronic newsroom systems

News production has to overcome special challenges which are assisted by the use of electronic newsroom systems (ENS) a fancy name for a computer system.

Information coming into a newsroom (stories, or 'wires', satellite feeds etc.) needs to be seen by a great many people. Running orders (the order in which the stories will appear in the final programme) will change right up to transmission, and often while the programme is on air. Computers are ideally suited to disseminating information.

Journalists usually receive the wire stories from major news providers (e.g. Reuters, AP etc.) on the computer. They write a script on the computer, normally in two halves – a VT package and a studio link. The studio link is fed directly onto a prompter on the front of the presenter's camera.

The VT part of the script is edited together. The computer automatically times the link duration (and can allow for slow or fast readers), adds up all the VT durations, advertisement breaks etc., and gives a constantly updated total programme duration.

Additionally, an archive of background information and a store of stories and pictures that have gone to air is available, a vital resource for journalists.

Dumb terminals and PCs

ENS used to have a powerful computer (mainframe) in the middle of a network with rows of dumb terminals hanging onto it. This worked adequately, but there were things it couldn't do. For example, some people wanted to create good-looking letters. Others wanted to store finance information. Scheduling was important to a further group. The ENS wasn't very good at any of these.

Another problem facing users was that systems would sometimes slow down, usually at critical times (just before transmission). This was because everyone wanted to use the computer at the same time, and the network connecting all the terminals together was being hammered.

The obvious answer is to use personal computers (PCs). There is still a central machine (a server) which holds the shared information (wire stories, running orders etc.). But now if you want to create fancy letters you use a word processor on your own PC. If you are interested in finance, there are several excellent financial packages available.

Network traffic – the amount of information being passed between the PC and the server – is greatly reduced, as most of the computing is done by the separate desktop machines.

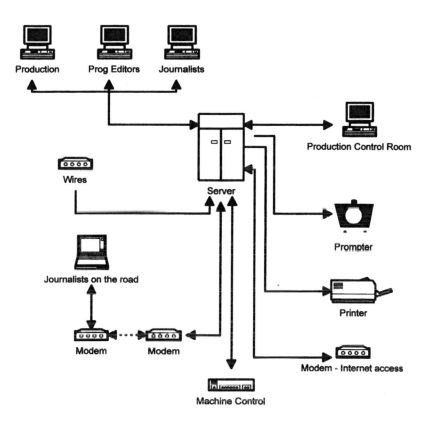

Production Prog Editors Journalists

Production Control Room

Wires

Server

Prompter

Journalists on the road

Printer

Modem Modem

Modem - Internet access

Machine Control

Simplified electronic newsroom system

Using computer systems

The running order

Just like a paper running order, this shows the order in which we expect the stories to appear 'on air'. There may be legitimate reasons why the order needs to change – OBs might not be ready, VTs could be stuck in edit suites, live guests may not have turned up. These are typical problems news teams face each day.

Most news programmes are live, so if something goes wrong you can't stop and talk about it – quick decisions need to be made, and those decisions passed on to everyone concerned.

It is vital directors are aware of alterations in running orders, and pass the changes down talkback. Not everyone will have a display in front of them, and those who do may not have noticed a change.

Customised displays

Some advanced ENS give different displays to different people, depending on the information they need to see. For example, a production assistant will be very interested in timing a programme, and may want to see lots of timing information. The graphics operator will want to see the same running order, but see graphics requirements instead. They are both looking at the same story order, but automatically receive different displays.

Scripts

Most ENS lay out scripts in a fairly traditional style. It's really important that everyone is consistent on layout, as you may need to extract information from the script at high speed. You may start a programme before the end has been written, a common situation in breakfast television, where some news won't even have happened before you go on air.

When you come to a news segment three hours after going on air, you may look at the script for the first time just seconds before it is the current story.

GIGO (garbage in, garbage out)

For all timing calculations the ENS is completely dependent on information given to it by humans. If you feed it the wrong duration for a VT package, it will give you the wrong programme duration.

WinCueNet
Production with precision

VT Ops Layout

Start Time 10.00.00
End Time 10.30.00
Show +/- 0.03.00

ID	Story Title	VT	Edit Suite	Format	SOT	Status	Hittime
1	Live Pre-titles	PT001	Tx Shelf	SP	0.20	Ready	10.00.00
2	Hello and menu	Menubg1	Tx Shelf	DVC	0.00	Ready	10.00.32
3	Snowboarding	5302	Ed 7	Profile	3.20	Ready	10.00.52
4	Snowboarding B/A				0.00		10.04.37
5	Cookery Demo				4.10		10.04.47
6	Into Break	5634	Ed 3	DVC	0.10	Cutting	10.09.17
7	AD BREAK				2.30		10.09.43
8	Out of Break	PT002	Tx Shelf	SP	0.00	Ready	10.12.13
9	Handover to news				0.00		10.12.20
10	Inflation Crisis	5991	Ed 5	DVC	1.20	Cutting	10.12.25
11	Minister resigns	5513	Ed 6	Profile	1.12	Writing	10.14.00

The Magazine Show | Wires - Urgent | Eight O'clock News | Basic Studio Directing
For Help press F1   English   Idle   NUM   Mem 91,148 KB
Start | WinCue Database Server | WinCue Layout Editor | Client - [Basic Studio...

_ File Edit Rundown Story Transmission Tools Window Help

WinCueNet
Production with precision

Directors Layout

Start Time 10.00.00
End Time 10.30.00
Show +/- 0.03.00

ID	Story Title	Talent	VT	Link	SOT	Est	Act	Hittime
1	Live Pre-titles		PT001	0.12	0.20	0.30	0.32	10.00.00
2	Hello and menu	L & D	Menubg1	0.20	0.00	0.20	0.20	10.00.32
3	Snowboarding	L	5302	0.25	3.20	4.00	3.45	10.00.52
4	Snowboarding B/A	L		0.10	0.00	0.10	0.10	10.04.37
5	Cookery Demo	D & J		0.20	4.10	4.30	4.30	10.04.47
6	Into Break	L	5634	0.16	0.10	0.20	0.26	10.09.17
7	AD BREAK				2.30			10.09.43
8	Out of Break		PT002	0.07	0.00	0.10	0.07	10.12.13
9	Handover to news	L & D		0.05	0.00	0.05	0.05	10.12.20
10	Inflation Crisis	P	5991	0.15	1.20	1.30	1.35	10.12.25
11	Minister resigns	P	5513	0.17	1.12	1.30	1.27	10.14.00

The Magazine Show | Wires - Urgent | Eight O'clock News | Basic Studio Directing
For Help press F1   English   Idle   NUM   Mem 91,148 KB
Start | WinCue Database Server | WinCue Layout Editor | Client - [Basic Studio...

Courtesy Autocue

One running order, two different displays

Machine control software (1)

Staffing is the biggest cost most studios face, so there is not surprisingly considerable interest in automated systems that help reduce the number of people needed to put out a live programme.

One way this has been tackled has been through machine control software (MCS) – using electronic newsroom systems to replace some studio operations. Some applications have worked very well. Others have yet to prove their worth. A few are a complete nightmare.

Caption generators

This is without doubt one of the success stories of MCS. Instead of writing a name down on a piece of paper, rushing to a capgen operator and screaming at him to type it up instantly (OK, so maybe I'm a little harsh on hacks, but I've seen it happen), the journalist types the caption information directly into his computer script. They will usually be offered a menu of styles, for example, two line supers, single line, etc. to choose from. They then just type in the caption text.

In the production control room a list of captions is stripped out of the running order. They are automatically generated in order with the ENS telling the caption generator machine what font to use, the size, layout and text information.

This has the added benefit of accuracy. The one person who should have all the correct caption information is the journalist. If he types it into the ENS correctly, that's how it will come out on screen.

Prompters

This was the first device to be attached to an ENS, and most are able to keep track of the latest version of stories. Some ENS need stories to be 'downloaded' into the prompting device, which can be a useful safety device, but it is also slower to receive changes.

VT

Just because it can be done doesn't necessarily mean it should be done. Attaching VT machines to an ENS is possible but only suits certain operations. If there are unlikely to be many story order changes, or changes always happen early then it works just fine. However, if anything goes wrong with the computer system you are totally stuffed. Also, if someone moves the wrong stories around, albeit only for a second, your VT machines will eject all the tapes they have lined up.

There is nothing more painful than watching a tape machine lace up when you desperately need a VT. It seems to take forever.

Courtesy Sony

Cart systems can usually be connected to newsroom computers for tapes to be automatically queued up for transmission.

A robot arm pulls the requested tape from a stack and loads it into one of the VTRs.

The machines need to be able to 'talk to each other', in other words the cart machine has to be able to tell the newsroom system if a VT is missing. This information should then appear on the newsroom system displays.

Carts can either be directly controlled, i.e. if the programme editor changes the story order then the cart will immediately follow those changes, or a running order can be 'downloaded' into a cart system and then the connection to the newsroom system broken. This is effective if you have many tape numbers to load, but ultimately want a human making the decisions about which tape is to appear in which machine.

Machine control software (2)

Stills store

This works in a very similar way to the capgen. A reference number is put into the running order that matches the stills store memory. During the programme a list is built up of the stills, and you simply hit a button to call up the next one when you are ready.

Laser disk

This works well. Laser disks have been used primarily for keeping regular graphics and stings required for programmes. The quality of the pictures remains permanently high, and the ENS can cue up requested segments very quickly.

Non-linear systems

This is the direction in which most news studios are heading. Ultimately, instead of using VT machines, all edited packages will either be loaded into, or cut directly on, a non-linear device.

Instant access means changes can be made very quickly without leaving the director in the lurch. Be aware that there are difficult issues to be faced with large non-linear systems, primarily to do with housekeeping. Someone has to decide what stories to chuck out to make space for the new ones.

Cameras

There is no reason why robotic cameras could not be connected to an ENS. Few have found this to be beneficial.

Lighting

Lighting changes (typically at the beginning or end of a show) can be programmed into an ENS, as long as the lighting controller has a method of receiving instructions. Note that this is not the same as automatically setting levels, and an ENS will generally be unaware of the skin colour of a presenter or guest, and the implications for lighting levels.

Accuracy

If information typed into newsroom systems is one letter wrong, the machine control software will not work. Tape/disk recorders will not line up the right stories, captions will not appear, stills stores will offer the wrong picture, directors will get very upset.

If there is any part of the above sentence that you do not understand, please get clarification from someone who does. Before it's too late.

140

Courtesy Autocue

Displays like this will become more and more commonplace for directors. This one shows VT clips being automatically offered up by a disk recorder in the order demanded by an electronic newsroom system.

Automated control rooms

Having seen how the roles of many operators can be partially run by computers, studios are beginning to appear that are built around their newsroom and automation systems. They use just two operators during the busy parts of the day, reducing to one in the quiet spells.

Technical directors

In control rooms with just one or two people there clearly is no place for a director who has no actual operational role. These new studios use one technical director and a sound supervisor, or two technical directors who swap roles after a few hours.

The technical director directs the programme, and also vision mixes. Additionally he may control robotic cameras, stills stores and other vision sources. There will without doubt be a demand for directors who are operationally proficient and highly computer literate in the future.

Automation limits

The computer system takes care of the bulk of programme timings, and is able to count out of 'VTs'. I use the term 'VTs' somewhat loosely here – there is often no video tape involved, the packages appearing on a video server. The countdown is provided by an electronic sampled voice and automatically warns the control room as the package is coming to an end.

Transmission suites are being dispensed with, as it is almost as easy for the studio to play out all presentation inserts (ads, promos etc.) directly from the same video server.

The level of automation can be set right up to the point where it will automatically cut back to the studio when a story finishes. It will put captions on screen at pre-programmed times without anyone pushing a button.

It is possible on modern newsroom systems to pre-program which camera to use on each link, along with the type of shot; however, this has been found by some people to be automating for the sake of it, and it is much easier for the technical director to decide quite late what shot to use and select it on the pre-set bank of the vision mixer. The computer will then just cut to the pre-set bank when the package finishes.

A relaxed-looking Gavin Esler (presenter) in front of the BBC News 24 control room. Two technical directors fulfil the operational roles while directing the programmes.

Arguably the programme editor doesn't need to be in the control room, as long as the running order is complete and comprehensive.

Most countries with high labour costs are looking to reduce studio staffing requirements, and we can expect all directors in the future to need operational skills.

Directing for real

Your first 30 seconds in a studio will have the most impact on the entire crew. Get this right, and everyone will bend over backwards to help you throughout the day.

Give the people what they need

The presenter and producer need to hear someone they believe will be able to hold the programme together if it all goes horribly wrong.

Technical crews will give a director anything he wants, but expect the director to understand what is, and what is not, possible. Know what you want before you go into the studio, and find out beforehand if you are asking for the impossible.

Be positive

Everyone listens and reacts to the director. If you go into a studio and are positive and full of energy, most crews will feed off that and give you the results you need. This isn't always easy – when you have been getting out of bed at 3.00 a.m. for six months, you may not feel overly human. Tough. Deal with it.

Confidence

Most people who are new to directing, and even old hands when faced with complicated programmes, are a bit nervous. Don't go around telling everybody. They're all concerned with their own nerves, but believe the programme will work because the director knows what he's doing.

Presenters want to be certain what they are doing next. Tell them.

Technical crews want to know what the sources are. Be specific. It is not acceptable to say 'Roll VT' when you have six VT machines. Be precise. 'VT B, roll'.

Listen

You must take in information from other people during a programme. If the production assistant tells you the out words of a VT you should be listening for them, not just to the count. If the programme editor changes the order of the stories there is probably a really good reason for them to do so. Take in that change and pass it on clearly and at a time that suits the operators around you.

Pointing at monitors has been going on since the days that vision mixers consisted of a row of faders (when they cracked how to do mixes, they did lots of them).

While the machines have changed, the pressure of live television hasn't. Directors have always worked under intense deadlines, suffered the mortifying feeling of programmes collapsing underneath them, and held the studio together when everything conspired against them.

Dealing with presenters

Some presenters are notoriously difficult and unpleasant. However, the vast majority are perfectly reasonable and easy to get on with.

Why presenters can be difficult
Presenting can be a surprisingly lonely job. It sounds strange, but while the control rooms are often packed with people the presenter may be on the studio floor with just a floor manager.

When the presenter is on air the audience tends to forget there is a team behind them. If the programme falls to pieces, the presenter feels like they are left with egg on their face. Everyone else may feel dreadful, but the only person the audience knows is the presenter.

Meeting for the first time
If you have not worked with a presenter before, either get introduced or do it yourself. They will probably assume you have years of experience and know exactly what you are doing. I see little reason for correcting the misconception.

In the studio
There are two things above all else that presenters need to know. What story (or page) they are reading next, and to which camera.

When you give them this information, watch their reactions in your monitors. The vast majority of the time it is obvious whether or not they heard **and took in** what you said. If you are not convinced, repeat it.

Looking good every day
Most of us have the occasional late night. If we go into work looking less than our best, we don't get a significant percentage of the country's population saying how rough we look. Some presenters are particularly fussy over the choice of make-up artist and lighting director since, between them, they can take years off someone's appearance.

The biggest individual mistake we make in television is to try to keep people looking young. This starts off being tiresome, getting flattering lighting. It becomes harder (more expert make-up). After a decade or two it becomes virtually impossible.

There is nothing wrong with people growing older and there is nothing sadder than seeing someone trying to hang on to their youth. To blame the technical staff for someone looking their age is ridiculous.

If your presenters are having difficulty reading the prompter there are a number of options up your sleeve to help.

Can the display be made brighter? (The adjustment is usually on the prompting unit on the front of the camera.)

Would increasing the font size help?

Would reversing the image (black lettering on a white background) be clearer?

Failing these you may have to move the camera closer.

Rehearsals

Rehearsals should not be for the performers' benefit. They should have practised in rehearsal rooms – or any room frankly – without you paying the hourly rate for an entire studio crew and facility.

This will be the first time the crew have seen the production. They deserve the time to rehearse their own contribution to the programme, and if your plan doesn't work, you need time to work out another option and to rehearse that as well.

Get started

More time is lost at the beginning of a studio day than at any other period. You must get to the studio on time. If you fail to turn up, within a few days the rest of the crew won't bother being prompt, and you will never get the production completed on budget.

At the allotted time, sit down in front of your microphone and introduce yourself. You should already have met all the senior crew members, but the others may never have heard of you before. Say who you are and what programme you are doing.

Run a talkback check

Ask in turn if the floor manager, sound supervisor, graphics, VT and cameras can hear you. Cameras will reply by nodding up and down. If anyone doesn't respond, first find out if they are there. If not, get someone to find them (often the job of the technical co-ordinator), or get their headsets replaced if that is the cause of the problem.

Studio schedule

You should have distributed a proper plan of everything you are going to do that day in the studio. Be aware if you are wandering off the plan, it is hard to recover lost time later in the day.

Try out the plan

You will have prepared camera cards and a shooting script for most productions. This should form the bulk of the final programme, and while it is possible to make as many changes as you like, the more changes you make the less time you will have to rehearse and the messier everyone's scripts and shooting cards become.

Breaks and finishing

Crew meal breaks should begin and finish on time, and it's your fault if they don't. Many studios now impose massive financial penalties for production teams that overrun. It is no longer acceptable for directors to flounce around saying it was for artistic reasons – if the schedule was reasonable you should have achieved it.

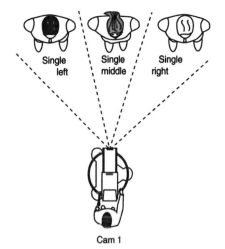

Single
left

Single
middle

Single
right

Cam 1

If you have a camera covering a number of people your instructions have to be clear and unambiguous. Using terms 'Single, left/middle/right' make it obvious which person you want on shot.

During rehearsals you must run through the terms and conventions you intend to use.

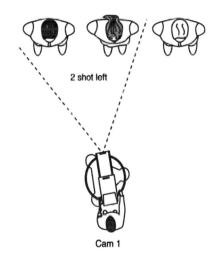

2 shot left

Cam 1

Similarly if you have a group of three do not call for a 2-shot without specifiying which.

1. You will be given the wrong one.
2. The crew will think you are stupid.

Call for a '2-shot left' or '2-shot right'.

149

Starting programmes

Stuffing up the start of a live programme is one of the most depressing ways to spend your day. No matter how brilliant you are for the rest of the show, it will be an imperfect programme.

Learn the format

Most programmes start the same way each time, with standard camera moves and often fixed VT machines for replays. Learn the format.

Typical starts

Let's look at a typical programme. It has opening titles which mix to a wide shot of the studio, a lighting change, camera zooms in to a tight 2-shot and presenters (two of them) speak alternately. As they tell the audience what's coming up in the programme there are pictures to match. At the end we mix through to the first presenter who has a window key (also known as an inset or, confusingly, OTS – over the shoulder).

Get ahead as far as you can

Check every source as far ahead as possible before you go on air. Get in the habit of checking your sources methodically – you will be less likely to miss something out. In this example:

Camera 1 offering wide shot (having checked the 2-shot he will finish on)
Camera 2 offering MS of presenter 1 allowing for window key
Camera 3 offering MS of presenter 2 allowing for window key

VT A offering opening titles on 10 second pre-roll (clock showing)
VTs B, C, D all offering their headline ulay VTs

Stills store 1A offering graphic for first story
Stills store 1B offering graphic for second story

Prompter offering start of programme

Titles

The world standard for opening titles is still a 10 second roll (i.e. 10 seconds before going on air you roll the tape). Picture should appear early (around −3 seconds on the clock). Sound must not start before zero.

Your clock will be visible to the transmission suite, and the continuity announcer will use it to finish their introduction exactly on time.

VT A


```
                        OPENING TITLES (VT A)
X Cam 1
WS Z/I to 2S
                    John
                    Good Evening and welcome to
                    'Regional Tonight', I'm John
                    Smith.

                    Anne
                    And I'm Anne Jones.  On
VT B                tonight's programme. . .

                    (ulay: H/L: M-Way Tragedy)
                    Motorway madness . . . more
                    lives are lost as drivers
VT C                ignore warnings of heavy fog.

                    John
                    (ulay:  H/L: Unemployment)
                    Unemployment down in the
                    region, but at what price?
                    Can you raise a family on the
VT D                minimum wage?

                    Anne
                    (ulay:  H/L Goal)
                    And in sport, a boost for
                    Regional United, as they score
                    their first goal in eleven
Cam 2               games.
Wkey John
                    John (i/v)
                    But first . . . the warnings
                    have been sounded a hundred
                    times, but still motorists
                    choose to ignore them.  And
                    today . . .
```

151

Getting 'on air'

The tricky mouthfuls

In the example given, having to say

'Mix 1 … zoom 1 … up lights … dip music, and cue John.'

is what usually trips up new directors. Learn it by rote, say it clearly and you will have plenty of time.

Know where your sound is coming from

We often run music under opening sequences, and that sound may well come from the same tape as the opening titles (in this case VT A). We obviously need to let VT A run right through to where John is starting his introduction to the first story. Just because you are not taking the pictures does not mean you can eject a VT.

The first machine likely to become free is VT B (as soon as its headline underlay is clear). The VT for your top story is likely to come from this machine.

Complicated sequences

On large programmes it is not unusual to be running an eight-tape sequence combined with graphics and music. While this sounds like hard work for the director, it is even harder for the VT/sound operators.

Pre-record if necessary

The importance of a clean start cannot be overemphasised. Many broadcasters will not risk complicated opening sequences falling flat on their faces, and insist on pre-recording the start of programmes.

While this might sound a little wimpish, if the viewers can't tell then all you are doing is preventing yourself from looking stupid.

Rehearse, but not too late

Obviously if you are going live with a tricky title sequence you will want to rehearse. The big warning here is don't rehearse too late.

If you have just one minute before going on air, you will be better off doing it for the first time live and unrehearsed, but knowing everything is ready and lined up, rather than rehearsing (for your sake) but making the VT operator's life impossible, needing to recue many tapes at the same time as rolling others.

Director says:

"Standby titles off VT A."

"VT A . . . roll"
"Coming to Camera 1 on a mix. . .
   . . .and mix . . .

OPENING TITLES (VT A)

. . . zoom 1 . . . up lights. . . dip
music, and cue John."

John
Good Evening and welcome to
'Regional Tonight', I'm John
Smith.

"Cue Anne. Coming to VT B "

Anne
And I'm Anne Jones.   On

"VT B roll . . . and cut."

tonight's programme. . .

(ulay: H/L: M-Way Tragedy)
"Coming to VT C."

Motorway madness . . . more
lives are lost as drivers

"VT C roll . . . and cut . . cue John."

ignore warnings of heavy fog.

John
(ulay: H/L: Unemployment)
"Coming to VT D."

Unemployment down in the
region, but at what price?
Can you raise a family on the

"VT D roll. . . and cut . . cue Anne."

minimum wage?

Anne
(ulay: H/L Goal)
"Coming to John, camera 2 and
Stills Store 1A, story 1, 'Motorway
Accident."

And in sport, a boost for
Regional United, as they score
their first goal in eleven

"Fade music, mix 2 and cue John"

games.

John (i/v)
But first . . . the warnings
have been sounded a hundred
times, but still motorists
choose to ignore them.   And
today . . .

Finishing programmes

The ends of programmes tend to be set pieces, in many ways similar to the starts of programmes, but usually simpler.

Here we have another mythical programme – a sports chat show. At the end the presenter (Andy) will ad-lib a 'thank you' to the guest (Glen), before turning to his camera (camera 3) and reading off the prompter.

Pre-fade roll
This means running a tape of a known duration (or music from a separate source) at a fixed time before the programme needs to end. You can mix to this tape at any time after it has rolled, and you know it will have pictures and music that finish at exactly the right time. This is a useful technique for live programmes, but the tape has to be rolled at precisely the right time, even if you are busy with something else.

Headline recaps
(Not used in this example.)
Used in many news programmes as an 'elastic' item, the last story is often a recap of the top headlines. If the programme is slightly 'under' in duration (finishing too early) the presenter reads a few more headlines to take up the slack. If the programme is 'over' (finishing too late), they read just the top line. Make sure both you and your presenter know how many headlines need to be read and what the last one will be.

Promos
As is common in today's programming, there are two promos. One is for a football match the next day, and the other a plug for the programme the following week.

If you are planning to promote items at the end of your show, make sure you have spoken to presentation. It looks a bit silly if you spend the last two minutes of your show plugging another programme just to go straight into a trailer for it the moment you are off air.

Spreading time
Let the crew know whether there is time in hand or if it is all a bit tight. If you are coming out early, the camera crew can slow down the speed they zoom out and the lighting supervisor can slow down how quickly the lights fade. These two alone can eat a surprising amount of your excess time.

Other standard ways of stretching a programme is to repeat the promos, or to get your presenter to ad-lib extra details while they are out of vision. The programme producer should be able to give extra information into their earpiece to help fill any gap.

```
VT A PFR @ 1 min to Off
Air

Cam 3                                                        /
MCU Andy
                                   Andy
                                   (THANKS GLEN)
Cam 1                                                        /
MCU Glen

Cam 3                                                        /
A/B
                                   And that's all we have time
                                   for this week.  I'll be back
                                   with tomorrow's big match,
CG + VT B                          when  /

                                   Sevenoaks United take on
                                   Tonbridge Town for the
                                   Littlevalue Cup.  That's live
                                   here on A Sports Channel at
Cam 3                              2.00p.m., kick-off at 2.30.  /
A/B
                                   Next week Keith Krotchety
                                   will join us in the studio and
                                   we'll be finding out why he
                                   took up his new appointment at
                                   Forlorn Football Club.

                                   Until then,  from all of us
Cam 2                              here, goodbye.  /
2S Z/O to WS

Capgen credits                           /
Dur: 15 sec

SS: End Caption                          /
```

Typical end to a programme

Capgen over VT
In this example the promos are out of vision (OOV), and consist of a capgen over a VT background. This is also a common technique, having a long tape of a moving background which is appropriate for the programme, and placing large captions over the top of it.

Credit rollers
The only thing that really matters here is that you know exactly how long it takes for the credits to run through. You may need to finish them before a final caption appears (often a production company credit). Once credit rollers have started there is usually little you can do to speed them up.

Changing credits
Static credits are prepared on separate pages of the caption generator. This has the advantage that you can speed them up by changing pages more quickly. Again, be aware how long ideally you want them to run, and the minimum duration you need.

Crash credits
Used at the end of live programmes instead of a full credit sequence when the programme has overrun. This will often be just one page (presenter, producer, director) used over very short closing music.

Long tails for presentation
When you finish a programme, leave the last picture or caption up for a long time. If presentation are having any problems with their machines this looks a lot better than pictures going to tape shash. Do not let any sound leave the studio for at least a minute, in case this has been 'dribbled over' by presentation. (This is a technique that prevents reverb from being cut off too quickly at the end of a programme, but leaves your studio sound 'live to air' for longer.)

Count to off air
The production assistant will be counting the programme off air, and should also give a special count down to the point where the pre-fade roll closing titles need to be rolled. They will also normally be liaising with presentation, making sure they are aware that the programme is about to end.

Courtesy
Do not forget to thank the staff you have been working with when you have finished.

Director says:

"Standby closing titles off VT A, pre-fade roll."

(at 1 min to 'off air') "VT A . . . roll"
"Coming to Andy on Camera 3 . . .
 . . .Cut 3, cue Andy"

	Andy
"Coming to 1. . . and cut."	(THANKS GLEN)

"Coming to 3. . . and cut."

"Coming to Capgen over VT B. . ."	And that's all we have time for this week. I'll be back with tomorrow's big match, when
"B Roll. . . cut and animate capgen"	
"Coming back to Andy, Camera 3."	Sevenoaks United take on Tonbridge Town for the Littlevalue Cup. That's live here on A Sports Channel at
"Cut."	3.00p.m., kick off at 3.30.
"Fade music up underneath from VT A. Coming to Camera 2 on a mix with live capgen, standby to pull out. Standby credit roller. "	Next week Keith Krotchety will join us in the studio and we'll be finding out why he took up his new appointment at Forlorn Football Club.
"Mix . . . up music, and zoom out . . ."	Until then, from all of us here, goodbye.

. . . Dim lights, Go credits."

"Coming to final credit on Stills Store 1A clean on a mix,. . .

and mix."

(When music finishes)
"Fade sound."

"Thank you".

Talkback

Communication between the control rooms and the studio floor is through production talkback (PTB). Some studios have separate talkback systems for lighting and sound, but many have just the one system. Everyone involved with technical operations needs to be able to hear talkback clearly.

Production talkback

The microphone in front of the director is left open. It is assumed that directors (and production assistants who sit next to them) have so much to say that there is no point in switching it off.

An immediate caveat to new directors: assume that talkback is always live, and someone is always listening. Even if a studio is completely empty with the lights switched off, talkback also goes to other parts of the building (e.g. the transmission suites, central apparatus rooms etc.). If you have a personal phone call in front of the director's microphone, it won't be personal.

Microphone technique

The microphone level will have been set so that if you speak normally everyone can hear you clearly. Do not put your mouth right next to the microphone – that will distort the signal. Do not grab the microphone. Do not under any circumstances tap the microphone with your pen – it comes out as a loud thud to everyone on headphones.

Do not sing or whistle. It may sound wonderful to you, but the chances are it will annoy people on the receiving end, who will switch it off. This makes it somewhat harder for you to contact them.

Other people using PTB

Most other people can talk on the talkback circuit, but they have to switch their microphones on temporarily. Don't allow unnecessary chatter over talkback – it has been put there for the sole intention of making television programmes, not to assist social bookings.

Presenters talkback

Presenters listen to production talkback. It's either 'open', in which case they hear it the whole time, or it's 'switched', where the director has to press a button for the duration they want the presenters to hear. Find out which type of talkback your presenters prefer before starting your rehearsals, and make sure your production assistant is aware which system you are using for passing on programme timings.

The talkback panel at the back of this control room lets the news producer talk to any of the incoming sources (normally a reporter at a live location). There are individual volume controls for each incoming source, and the headphones prevent too much disturbance to the rest of the control room.

The producer can also speak to any of the presenters, who are each on separate circuits. This means he can speak to one without disturbing another who may be presenting at the time.

The panel in front of the programme director is virtually identical, except that the microphone is permanently turned on and connected to the production talkback (PTB) circuit, so that technical operators can always hear the director's instructions.

2- and 4-wires

If your studio has an outside broadcast it is usually impractical to run a cable with talkback to the production personnel at the location. The easy answer is to use cables that have already been laid throughout the country – which is where telephone companies come into the picture.

2-wires and 4-wires are, quite simply, telephone lines. For television communication a 2-wire normally sends talkback in one direction. If you want the person at the other end to be able to reply there needs to be a 2-wire running back. This combination of two 2-wires working as a pair is a 4-wire.

2-wires and 4-wires need to be booked. They are not instantly available, so make sure they have been arranged well in advance, normally at the same time as the main vision and audio circuits.

On some programmes the communications becomes the most complex part of the set-up. Sports programmes in particular tend to have lots of 2- and 4-wires. For example, if there is a live football match, there is a producer and a director back at the studio. There is also a director at the match, and a commentator. All need to be able to speak to each other.

Discipline

The more complex the communications, the more important it is for everyone to identify themselves on talkback circuits. There is no point in just saying 'Are you there?' down a microphone if the people receiving the question don't know who you are, who you're calling or where you're calling from.

Think before you speak on any talkback circuit. Again, I know it's obvious, but if you are under pressure to get something done quickly it's easy to forget that the person at the other end may also be busy. There is no point in trying to speak to an OB director if they are in the middle of a complex opening titles sequence.

Be concise and polite whenever possible. There may be other people queuing up to talk, so don't be too chatty, particularly when dealing with broadcasters who are providing 'pool' feeds (again, very common in sport, where a local company may provide pictures from an event which are being taken live by many territories).

Having said that, taking just a couple of seconds to be friendly and helpful does make television much more pleasant to work in, and you are then more likely to find people willing to help you out if you need a hand.

The receiving end of talkback circuits are often outside broadcast units. The chances are they will be working in much more cramped conditions than the main studio, they may have their own rehearsals to run through and it may be pouring with rain outside. Don't be surprised if it takes them a few moments to respond to your talkback requests.

Clean feeds

You have a presenter on live location. Your studio presenter needs to be able to talk to them as part of your programme. You can't just turn the television on at the location to let them hear what's happening – you would get an echo at best, or complete 'howl-round' if the volume was too loud. So you give them an earpiece plugged into a TV instead, listening to their own live programme. However, when they start speaking they hear themselves coming back 'off air' into their ear, but with a slight delay. It takes only a couple of seconds before they come to a grinding halt. Not good.

PCF a.k.a. mix minus
What your OB presenter really wants to hear is everything going on in your studio, all your VTs, but not themselves. So the sound department puts together a special mix just for them. This is sent either down a 2-wire, or it can be fed into a phone line and picked up through a phone adapter into an earpiece. This is programme clean feed (PCF), also sometimes known as mix minus.

Interrupt fold back (IFB)
The system works fine. Your presenter can hear everything in your programme apart from themselves. The problem you face is being able to talk to them, to let them know how long it is until they are on air, or to tell them of any change in the programme schedule.

The solution is for the sound department to loop the PCF through a switch in front of the director. Normally the switch lets the signal go straight through, but if you press the switch it instead sends your microphone to the OB presenter's ear. This is known as interrupt foldback (IFB).

It would obviously be disastrous if your switch was left open, as the OB presenter would not be able to hear when the studio presenter introduced them, so this is usually done with a switch that cannot be latched.

Multiple clean feeds
Election night comes along. Now you have a number of presenters on OBs. They each need to hear each other, but not themselves. Now the sound department has to put together special mixes for each of them.

In the diagram, presenter A is in the studio with guests 1 and 2. They needs to hear the VTs and presenters B, C and D. Presenter B wants to hear presenter A and guests, VTs, presenters C and D, but not himself. Presenter C wants to hear VTs, presenter A and guests, B and D but not himself. And so on. On nights like this you want a really good sound supervisor.

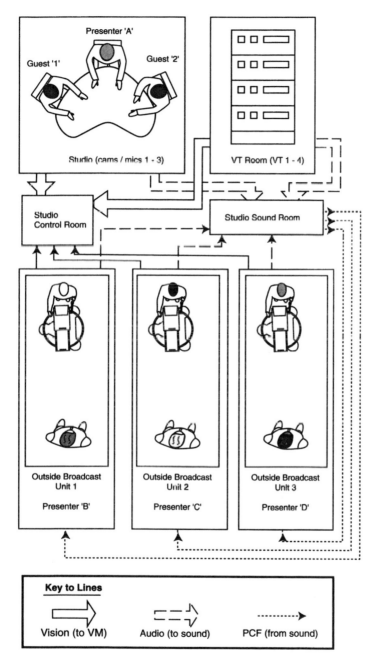

Presenter 'A'

Guest '1'　　　Guest '2'

Studio (cams / mics 1 - 3)

VT Room (VT 1 - 4)

Studio
Control Room

Studio Sound Room

Outside Broadcast
Unit 1

Presenter 'B'

Outside Broadcast
Unit 2

Presenter 'C'

Outside Broadcast
Unit 3

Presenter 'D'

Key to Lines

Vision (to VM)　　　Audio (to sound)　　　PCF (from sound)

Simplified circuits for three outside broadcast units

Communicating with live injects

A live outside broadcast (OB), whether it is a multi-camera affair or a more modest single camera unit, feeding into a studio is known as an inject. They are simple to work if you have good communications. Without good communications they will go belly up and you will be blamed.

PCF and PTB
Ideally the OB presenter is listening to PCF (or IFB), and the camera operator hears production talkback (PTB). Don't forget the camera operator cannot see the shots in your studio, so if you want his shots to match yours, you will need to talk him through exactly what you want.

Getting through to an OB
Just because you can see an OB presenter on a monitor does not mean they are plugged in and listening to talkback. The sound department should let you know when communications have been established.

Seeing a picture does not mean you can use it. Is it synchronous? In colour? Up to technical specifications? Some studios use an engineering manager who can let you know when the technical side is ready.

You need a 'pre-fade listen' (PFL) of the OB. This simply means you can hear them before they have been put on air through the sound mixer. It is very useful if you can have a separate volume control for this PFL.

Generally you will have this turned down – you won't want to be disturbed during the rest of the programme by the goings on at the OB. If the presenter there wants to speak to you they should stand in front of their camera and wave their arms around. They may feel a bit silly, but it's a neanderthal technique that works.

If you see them doing this, speak to them. Either deal with their problem or tell them to wait because you are busy (but don't forget to get back to them when you can).

It is also very useful if they give a big thumbs-up in front of their camera when they're happy, or responding positively to you. It's easy for you to see that – it may be harder for you to hear them.

Check, check and check again
Warning: Talkback, 2-wires and 4-wires have a tendency to stop working after a while, so use your monitors to watch for reactions when you speak to an OB. If you give a one-minute warning and nobody reacts, then do not let the programme try to cross over to them until you have checked it. Also there is little point in checking out an OB thirty minutes before you come to it, as you will need to check it again much closer to transmission.

Adam Boulton delivers a live inject into Sky News. It is not uncommon for journalists and their crews to have to wait in the rain for several hours before their brief moment on screen.

Making live injects work

There is only one way to make sure the inject will work smoothly, and that is to run through all the variables before it goes to air. Even if a producer has already done so, find 30 seconds to go through it again. The person in front of the camera will be under enormous pressure and may have forgotten some detail, or the plan may have changed without anyone informing them.

Confirm exactly when you expect them to be on air. Remind them of the name of your presenter in the studio. Tell them the format of the item. Will it a be question and answer session ('John is at [location], John what did the Prime Minister say this morning?') or is it a straight throw ('Over to John at [location].')? Try to warn the OB presenter what the question will be – it stops the programme looking stupid if they don't know the answer.

Some companies like to have reporters live at locations leading into VTs. You must know exactly how they are going to finish their introduction as you have to roll the tape off the back of it. Find out precisely what they are going to say, and **write it down before you forget**.

At the end of the VT, are you cutting back to the studio or to the OB again? Be sure to let everyone know in advance, and as it happens be very clear who you are cueing. For example, as the VT finishes, say 'Coming to John at [location]. Cut and cue John'.

It sounds pedantic. It works. Sound, vision mixers and presenters love it.

As the time for the inject approaches, give them a countdown. It is particularly useful if you can give them a two- and a one-minute warning.

Single camera units may have limited power and choose to keep lights switched off until the last moment. It is entirely reasonable of you as a director to expect them to be switched on at one minute to on air. Don't worry about it before that as long as the OB has said they are happy.

Let the OB know if they will be in shot before they start speaking. This is very common – we often use 2-way boxes on screen as the studio presenter introduces the OB presenter. You don't want the OB camera operator checking their focus or making a last-minute adjustment to the exposure when you have already cut them to air.

Similarly at the end of an inject, the presenter at the OB should continue to look into the camera on a steady shot until you have cleared them. There is nothing worse than seeing someone taking off their microphone before you have cut off their picture.

The popularity of single camera units doing live injects increased as their sensitivity improved (needing fewer lights), and the size, weight and power consumption of the camera decreased.

Secret or undercover filming on video used to be ... tricky.

Studio engineering

Like it or not (and most of us don't) we work in a technically complex environment. Fortunately there are engineers and technicians around to sort out most of the problems, but it is important that we, as directors, understand a few of the basics of television.

The PAL television picture

PAL is the system used by Britain, Australia, India, Singapore and elsewhere. Other countries use a similar systems with a few important differences that we'll come to later.

A PAL picture is drawn on a television set by firing electrons at the phosphorous surface of the television tube, making it glow. It scans across the set, moves down and scans across another line until it reaches the bottom, drawing 312.5 lines. It then goes back to the top and draws another 312.5 lines between the first ones.

Each pass of 312.5 lines is a field. Fifty fields are drawn each second. Two fields make a complete frame, hence we get the 625 lines per frame and 25 frames per second.

Synchronous pictures

Suppose we turn on two cameras in a studio. They each start scanning a picture, but while Cam 1 is at the top of a field, Cam 2 may be near the bottom. If we were to cut or (worse still) mix between the two pictures there would be a horrible transition. The picture would roll, tear and generally look a mess.

To sort the problem out engineers send cameras and other pieces of equipment (e.g. VT, graphics) a synchronising signal. The cameras use this to work out when they should start scanning from the top.

So how does this affect us as directors? You might see a picture on a monitor in a gallery that looks fine. However, if the vision mixer or engineer tells you it's non-sync, **you cannot under any circumstances mix to it**. In an emergency it is possible to cut to the source, but you may have to justify your decision to the broadcasting authorities.

The quickest way round the problem is to use a frame store or synchroniser. This device takes in any non-sync signal, and feeds out the same signal, but synchronous with the studio. There is a slight delay in the picture – normally 1/25th of a second. Engineers can usually get pictures fed through a frame store within a couple of minutes … as long as the equipment is available.

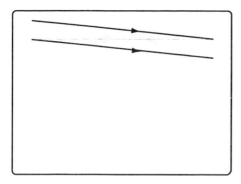

The electron beam draws a line across the screen from left to right, moving very slightly downwards (solid line). It then very quickly returns to the left hand edge of the screen (thin line) before drawing the next line.

One complete screen full of lines is a field.

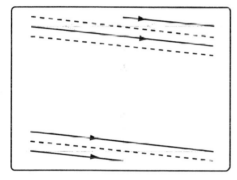

When the field is complete the electron beam moves very quickly back to the top of the screen, where it starts drawing lines (solid line) between the ones in the previous field (broken line).

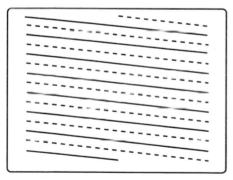

Having completed two fields of interlaced lines, the electron beam goes right back to the beginning to start drawing the next frame.

169

Television systems

Televisions across the world use slightly different systems. This is partly historical, partly political. NTSC, PAL and SECAM are the three main systems you'll hear about, although each have local variations.

America introduced colour television (NTSC) in the 1950s, a 525-line 30-frames per second system. The rest of the world watched and made a few modifications before introducing their own systems. SECAM, a 625-line system started in France in the late 1960s, about the same time that PAL was developed.

One of the main defining criteria of a national television system is the local electricity supply. American electricity has 60 cycles per second (Hz), so it was logical for them to use 60 fields/30 frames per second. The British, on the other hand, have only 50 Hz, so they use 50 fields per second for their PAL system.

Converters

For directors it means that tapes and live satellite feeds from other parts of the world cannot be put straight to air. Signals can be put through black boxes that convert them from one system to another, although there is a quality loss, and a slight delay to the signal.

The reason for the quality loss is that converters have to calculate how the picture should look between particular lines and frames.

Conversion generations

Where this loss becomes critical is when a signal has passed through more than one converter, which happens more often than we care to admit. It has become prevalent as television companies across the world exchange pictures on a daily basis (news and sport getting bounced around the world the most).

Widescreen

Many people would like us to switch to a widescreen format – the most common being 16:9 (from the current 4:3). This suits drama and films but has little benefit for talking-heads shows. The cost of replacing all television production equipment and receivers would boost the sales bonuses of some companies more than a tiny bit.

HDTV

High definition television has been developing for years without getting universal acceptance. Typically (I say typically because there are a number of different systems) there are just over a thousand lines on the screen, instead of 625 for Pal or 525 for NTSC. This is also a widescreen format.

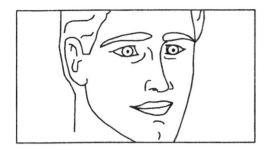

Big Close Up (BCU)
The 16:9 ratio suits showing films which are usually shot on a wider format than television. Shot composition changes as you try to get rid of excess 'space' around your subject.

2 Shot (2S)
2-shots are easier on the wider format, allowing more sensible spacing and a chance to show the background (a front-on 4:3 ratio 2-shot would need the subjects closer together).

Medium Shot (MS)
The main dificulty for multi-camera shooting (where you can't set up one shot at a time) is getting clean single shots. To get rid of unwanted shoulders etc. you may end up shooting very tight.

Widescreen format

Digital versus analogue television

Television signals used to be recorded in an analogue format. That simply means the signal could be of any value from 0 to 1 volt.

Whenever you pass an electronic signal down a wire, through a connector, into another machine, recorded onto tape, etc., it loses some quality – the signal becomes slightly distorted, and it is impossible for the receiving machine to work out exactly what the original signal looked like.

Once a tape had been copied a few times, that quality loss (generation loss) became apparent, so we tried not to copy tapes too often.

Ones and zeros

The other way of sending a signal is to take thousands of measurements, and send a series of binary numbers down a cable. So, if at a particular time the picture signal was 0.5 V, it would be converted to a series of '1s' and '0s' that, in binary terms, represents 0.5.

Now we send this new signal down a slightly grubby cable, through a seriously dodgy couple of connectors and onto another tape. By this stage our signal has again picked up a whole bunch of distortion and noise.

However, even covered in this mess it's obvious which bits were meant to be '1s', and which '0s'. So the receiving machine reconstructs the signal as a perfect copy of the original. Now, theoretically at least, we can copy from machine to machine, without ever losing any quality.

Compression

The problem everyone faces when dealing with digital signals is that they are huge. You need a massive computer memory to remember even a small video clip, so engineers have 'compressed' images.

For example, the difference between two successive television frames is actually very small. So if, instead of storing a complete new picture for every frame, you simply store the difference between two successive frames, that information would take up much less space in a computer memory.

There is a limit to how much you can compress pictures, after which you really notice the quality loss on screen, and we need to be particularly careful of compressing pictures that have already been compressed – they can end up a real mess.

Transmission

It's possible to transmit many digital television channels in the space that was used by a few analogue channels, so broadcasters are keen to move over to digital transmission systems. There are additional benefits to the viewers – they should receive better quality pictures, as long as the digital signal has not been compressed too much by the broadcaster. Viewers need either digital decoders attached to their old televisions, or new television sets.

First generation analogue signal

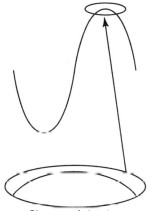

Close up of signal

The same part of the signal once it has been copied a few times

0 1 1 0 1 0 0 1 0 1 1 0 0 1 1 1 0 0

A digital signal. This can only consist of either a high voltage (represented by '1') or zero volts (represented by '0')

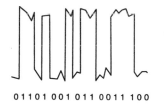

0 1 1 0 1 0 0 1 0 1 1 0 0 1 1 1 0 0

Even if the digital signal gets badly distorted it is still clear which bits are meant to be '1s' and which bits are '0s'. So a perfect copy of the original signal can be reproduced and recorded no matter how many times it is copied.

173

Satellites and microwaves

We regularly cover live events on television, and while many countries have extensive networks capable of sending pictures back to broadcasters, that is often impractical and an alternative method is needed.

Microwaves

The easiest, quickest and cheapest method is to use a microwave link. This means the live camera or VT machine at the location is fed into a transmitter that is aimed towards a receiving dish. Microwave aerials are small, and are often mounted on the roofs of small vans.

Microwaves suffer from one major drawback – the receiving dish needs a direct view of the transmitting aerial. If there is a hill in the way the signal will not get through. Given a clear 'line of sight' microwave signals can travel for as far as they can see.

However, it is possible have a series of links that 'hop' the signal to its final destination.

Satellites

Sometimes the outside broadcast will be at a place that would require a silly number of microwave links. At this point it becomes more economical to use a satellite. This involves sending the signal straight up towards a satellite in geo-stationary orbit, where it is picked up and sent back to a receiving station on the ground.

If you've ever tried to get a signal out from a city centre surrounded by skyscrapers you'll know it is often easier to use satellites than microwaves.

Satellites are more expensive. Typically you hire them for a minimum 10 minutes, then by additional 5-minute time slots. It is difficult to give prices as so many variables come into the equation (bulk bookings, destinations, distances etc.), but as a guide you'll pay around US$500 for the first 10 minutes, then $15 per minute after that. The point here is this stuff isn't cheap, so be ready with your VTs/OBs when the lines come up (i.e. you are connected through the satellite). Don't overrun.

Satellite up-link dishes are much bigger than micro-wave dishes, and, while they can be mounted on trucks, they are not subtle.

Alternatives

If you don't need to send pictures in real time (i.e. you are not doing a live link), then you can use a 'store and forward' device. This loads the pictures and sound into a computer memory, and uses much smaller satellites to send the pictures back to base. It takes a lot longer (typically 20 minutes to send a 2-minute piece) but it's much cheaper to hire these data satellite links, and the original transmitting station uses a small satellite phone dish, which is more practical to carry around.

Satellite uplink dishes are usually transported already assembled and are simply swung out of the truck and pointed (accurately) at the appropriate satellite. It is also possible to transport them in pieces, although this usually involves copious flight cases and a major excess luggage budget.

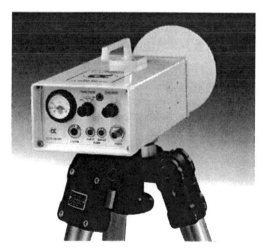

Microwave links are much smaller and simpler, and can be mounted on basic tripods.

Apart from being much cheaper they can also, if necessary, be powered by a car battery.

Live television

This scares a few directors, with some justification. If you make a mistake, it is a very public error.

There are good reasons for doing programmes live. It is usually cheaper – there is no post-studio editing cost, although you may need some for preparing studio inserts. It is also quick, and the vast majority of programmes finish on time.

Preparing for live transmission
As a director you must be aware of the on-air time, and work your rehearsal and meal breaks to accommodate.

Most of the additional work will be done by the PA and technical director. The PA will liaise with presentation to confirm transmission time and duration. They will do a clock and talkback check.

The technical director will make sure the audio and vision are getting to transmission control to the correct technical standard. You will lose your vision mixer for a minute or so at some stage while the TD runs through a couple of checks.

Cue dots
Some countries run a system of placing a small mark, or 'cue dot', in the top corner of the screen just before a live programme. Others use the cue dot on programme tapes to warn presentation that there is about to be a commercial break. The timing of the cue dot appearing and disappearing varies between organisations, but typically it comes on 30 seconds before the programme is to begin (or the ad break), and goes off at –5 seconds.

Off-air monitor
You should always have a monitor showing you what the channel is broadcasting. You can see when you are on air and when you are clear at the end of the programme.

Directing your way out of mistakes
If something goes wrong, you must make instant decisions. Be clear if it is a minor error and you are going to stick to the rehearsed plan. If it requires a major change, state which presenter is to read what story, to which camera.

Do not under any circumstance start a post-mortem before you are off air. It is unprofessional and will only make matters worse. Your job is to provide a clear direction for everybody to follow. Slow everybody down, clean up the mistake and make sure you don't tumble from one error to another.

Reacting to Fire Alarms

Many studios are equipped with two levels of fire alarms.

Level 1 (silent, flashing red light in the control room)

A fire alarm has triggered in the building or complex.

Action – Studio not On Air :
If you are not 'live', then empty the studio and control rooms, and go to the appropriate safety zones.

Action – Studio Live :
Technical Director should immediately find out how serious the problem is.

Warn the Floor Manager, who will clear the floor of members of the public and any disabled persons. The studio staff will be expected to help out with any evacuation of a studio audience.

The floor manager will close off any gas supply to the studio floor and remove any potential hazard that might get in the way of an evacuation.

Warn Presentation you are seeing a fire alarm, and tell them to standby to take you off air.

If possible reduce crewing level, typically one presenter, one cameraman, floor manager (no assistant floor managers), producer, director (no vision mixer, no capgen, no graphics) one sound supervisor (no assistants) one Technical Director (no lighting, no vision assistant), one V T operator.

Level 2 (audible, big flashing lights)

Your studio is on fire.

Tell presentation to take you off air immediately. Clear the studio, control rooms and any other local areas (make-up, changing rooms etc.).

Do not risk injury and lives for the sake of a television programme.

Editorial collapses

The worst that can happen in a live programme is a complete breakdown of the editorial running order. It can, if not stopped, cause the domino effect, where one item collapses, causing the next to collapse, which knocks down the next, and so on.

The domino effect

The example opposite shows a perfectly reasonable running order for the first part of a half-hour news programme, running on a commercial network. Allowing for adverts, the programme editor has just 24 minutes to fill, so he has broken it down into two parts of 13 and 11 minutes each.

The programme starts fine, with titles and a series of headlines. While the headlines are on air, the technical director tells you and the programme editor that the live link to the political rally is not ready and will be another five minutes.

The editor pushes stories 3 and 4 down the running order to accommodate.

The producer of the health scare story tells the editor that Dr Cwoat isn't at the studio yet. He isn't expected until 8.05 – having been told the interview would take place after that.

Stories 5, 6 and 7 all get bumped down.

Story 8 is now the top story. But the journalist working on the train strike story had been told he had until 8.10 to finish the edit. There is still a 'black hole' in the tape where some graphics are to be dropped in.

That leaves the editor with one 30-second story to run before the commercial break. Of course he could pull up some stories from the second half, but he is now leading on stories that did not appear in his headline sequence.

This is a bit of an extreme example, but most experienced directors have faced smaller scale versions.

Breaking the cycle

The answer is to break the cycle early by realising you are approaching a catastrophe. Run story 3, Political Rally VT. During the VT try to get the link up. If you can't, the presenter can say that they will be going live to the rally later in the programme. That 2 minutes 30 seconds gives you lots of time to sort out your options.

```
Mythical news at 8          Running order
```

No:	Story Name:	VT:	Dur:	Time:
1	Opening Titles	A	0.30	8.00.00
2	Headlines	B, C, D	0.45	8.00.30
3	Political Rally VT	A	2.30	8.01.45
4	Live at Pol. Rally		1.30	8.03.15
5	Health Scare VT	B	1.30	8.05.45
6	St Intv: Dr Cwoat		3.00	8.07.15
7	Helpline Number		0.30	8.10.15
8	Train Strike VT	C	1.45	8.10.45
9	Road Chaos Ulay	D	0.30	8.12.00
10	Pre-com Ulay	A, B	0.15	8.12.30
	Commercial Break		2.30	8.13.00

First half running order of news programme

Technical disaster

Machines break down. Fact. That means if you direct enough live programmes at some stage a machine will let you down. For a recorded programme this is annoying and can mess up your schedule. If you are 'live', it can give you a heart attack.

The 'What if ...' game
The theory goes like this. If you've sat down and worked out what you would do for every possible technical breakdown, or better still had someone throw theoretical problems at you, and you've worked out how to handle them, then when they happen for real you will know exactly what to do. So, in your spare time, play the game.

What do you do?
1. You make a decision.
2. You tell everybody what you want to do.
3. When everyone is ready you recover from the problem as cleanly as possible and move on.
4. You work around the machine until it is fixed.

All this sounds obvious, but each point needs to be done in order and with cold professionalism.

Making a decision
Do not just sit there looking at the problem. Do you want to stay with the machine or pull out? In a moment we'll go through some of the possible breakdowns you can face, the basic factors you must consider in making your decision and some of the options available.

Tell everybody
When things go wrong people react in one of two ways. They either remain absolutely silent (the correct response, as long as they have made sure you are aware of the problem), or they yell down talkback.

You must get silence. Everyone needs to hear what you want to do, so shut everyone up as fast as you can (rudeness/aggression is acceptable). Say what you want without rushing. Be clear, be precise.

A clean recovery
Do not blunder from one disaster to another. You must avoid crashing out of a VT back to a presenter who doesn't know what to do next, with a microphone still closed, and the sound of the broken VT machine still going to air.

Studio discipline can be very dull to enforce, until someone accidentally knocks a cup of coffee into one of the cameras.

Machine breakdowns

VT

Probably the most common machine to give you short notice problems. What you do depends on the severity of the breakdown. VT errors range from a few flashing green lines to complete loss of picture and sound.

The decision to stay with it or 'crash out' depends on how bad the picture is (can the audience clearly hear and see the story?) along with the importance of the story (if it is the top story and your next two VTs have to run off the back of it you will want to stay with it if possible).

If you decide to come out of the VT early go through the standard routine. Let everyone know what you are going to do, fade the sound from the outgoing tape, mix through to the presenter, apologise and cue on.

Graphics

This can be serious for programmes that use chroma-key (which includes many news programmes). If you lose the stills store you may have nothing to put behind your presenter. For this reason it is vital that you have a separate standby background available from a completely independent source. This could easily be a VT machine offering a static frame.

Cameras

It is unusual to lose multiple cameras, so simplify the range of shots you want and work around the one that is missing. Cameras themselves don't break down very often, although cable faults are quite common.

If you have to change the presenter's camera, be aware if it doesn't have a prompter unit on the front.

Capgen

Editorially captions are very important. If possible the presenter should 'back announce' who was on the tape. Short and sweet, please, 'Peter Strop MP talking to us earlier today.'

Vision mixer

Most studios are equipped with an emergency bypass switcher. This allows you to do simple cuts between primary sources (cameras, VT, SS etc.). It means you cannot usually do any chroma-keying, or put captions up, but it will get you through a programme. Be aware and warn everybody that cue lights on the cameras will not work.

Working around the problem

While carrying on directing you must also look ahead to see how the loss of a machine will affect the rest of the programme. Let the programme producer know in plenty of time if compromises need to be made.

Use the studio design to your advantage. Many studios have separate technical areas with windows, which reduces the noise level in the control room without cutting off the operators completely. If you are giving an instruction and you can see the person you will know immediately if they have heard and understood. A simple thumb up or down from the operator is a quick and effective response.

If something is going wrong, or people aren't responding when you expect them to, look to see if they have a problem. It's quicker than using talkback, and reduces unnecessary distractions to other operators.

Many studio floors are visible from control rooms. While it shouldn't be necessary to see the floor, occasionally it's useful to look over your shoulder and see what problems they are having.

Production errors

Rolling the wrong VT

A surprisingly easy mistake to make, particularly in a busy programme. The chances of this happening are greatly reduced if all tapes are clearly clocked, stating the story title and date. The vision mixer should always put the next tape on the preview monitor, so both of you can check it.

When it happens (sorry, 'if' it happens), immediately tell the presenter, sound and vision. Tell the presenter either to:

1. briefly reintroduce the correct VT or
2. go on to the next story.

Fade the sound from the wrong tape, then mix back to the presenter. Be aware that if you rolled the tape for the next story it will need to be recued.

Timing errors

If a VT finishes earlier than you expected, give an immediate 'Standby'. Quickly check that the presenter is not doing anything untoward, then cut and cue on.

This is one of the reasons for always putting the next source up on the vision mixer early.

No sound

If you cut to a source and there is silence, you must restate what source you are using. Do not say 'There is no sound'. That's the one thing the sound department already know. What they want to know is where it should be.

Within a couple of seconds they will either get the audio there, or tell you it is lost before it reaches the studio. In that case you have no choice but to crash out.

Vision mixing

If the VM presses the wrong button, it's usually pretty obvious. There is nothing you can do about it, and yelling at them will not make them perform any better – usually quite the reverse. State again clearly what you want, and if possible keep it simple. If they have been previewing all their shots you should have noticed that the wrong one was about to go to air.

Caption errors

You should always have a capgen preview monitor. Check spellings before putting up captions. You should notice, the VM should notice, the CG operator should notice.

© Sean Preston/GMTV Magazine

When errors happen on live programmes you usually have to make changes to the planned running order if you still want to fill the specified duration. Clear, accurate and calm decisions from the programme editors help smooth recoveries.

Presenting out of mistakes

Any presenter of a live programme should be able to handle an urgent correction or a breakdown at a moment's notice. How they react can make the difference between the programme looking professional, or as if it was made by a bunch of amateurs.

Correcting editorial errors

If an editorial mistake has been made in a VT, ideally the presenter will make an immediate correction. This reduces offence and legal liability. There are far too many possibilities to go through here, and it really affects programme editors more than directors. You need to know who is making the correction, and be clear they know which camera to use.

Each country has different publication legislation. Again, while this is an issue primarily for the programme editor, if anyone notices an editorial or legal mistake they should speak up.

Beating yourself up

The wording used on standard apologies varies from country to country, but the best reaction is short, polite and confident. You must acknowledge you have a problem, but please don't go on and on about it.

'We're sorry about the loss of that report – we hope to bring it to you later in the programme. In the meantime ...'

Staying with poor quality sound or pictures

If you have decided to stay on poor quality tape, then some acknowledgement that it was not up to professional standard should be made, otherwise it looks like you are happy to accept a low standard of television. Again the apology should be brief.

'We're sorry about the sound quality in that report. Sport now, and...'

Slowing the studio down

Often if something goes horribly wrong the control room needs a while to sort itself out. One of the vital skills in a presenter is to fill time. This is fairly easy when you have more than one presenter in the studio, but if they're on their own it's a little harder. Most magazine show presenters can talk about what will be coming up in the next few segments. News readers should always have a copy of the headlines with them. Sports presenters can normally talk for a couple of hours without any difficulty. Shutting them up can be challenging.

© Sean Preston/GMTV Magazine

The glamour of television as few viewers see it – working in tiny studios is common, particularly around centres of government, where television companies want to be able to do instant live injects without paying exhorbitant rent.

Presenters in these studios are often journalists who make regular contributions to programmes. Do not expect them to cope with the quantity of talkback or instant recovery that a full-time presenter should be able to handle.

188

Glossary

1 + 1 One plus one. One presenter plus one guest.

2 + 4 Two presenters plus four guests.

4-wire Bi-directional communications wire.

Analogue Signals that can have any value from 0 to 1 volt.

Angle of View The horizontal angle visible through a specific focal length lens.

Aperture correction (now known as 'detail') A way of electronically increasing the sharpness of a picture.

Backing track Instrumental recording replayed into a studio while a performer sings live.

Bars Electronically created test signal used to check (among other things) brightness (black level), contrast (white level) and colour.

BITC (pronounced 'bitsey') Burnt in time-code The time-code has been printed onto the vision and is always visible on screen. Used for taped off-line editing.

Black level The electronic level setting of the dark parts of a picture.

Bus A row of sources (e.g. on a vision mixer) usually placed in a row from which an operator can select an input.

Canting Twisting the camera on its axis through the lens, so the horizon is not parallel to the frame. Very MTV.

Capgen (CG) Caption generator. Creates type on screen, sending two signals – a video and a key.

CCD Charge-coupled device. The light sensitive device behind the camera lens that has replaced camera tubes. It converts the varying light levels into an electrical signal.

CCU Camera control unit. The base station for a studio camera. On this (or through a remote control panel) you can adjust all the camera and many engineering settings.

Chroma-key The technique of electronically removing one colour from a scene and replacing that part of the image with a different picture.

Chrominance The colour part of a signal showing hue and saturation.

Clearing cameras Letting cameras know you do not need them any more and they can move to a different area of the studio.

Control track Part of a VT recording used to maintain correct replay.

Complementary colour The colour which, if added to the original, will make white light.

Component A television picture kept in three separate parts. As the colour signals are not coded and later decoded the final picture is better quality, but three cables are needed to move a signal from one machine to another.

Composite A television picture that has the colour and luminance signals coded together, and which is sent down a single cable.

Crash zoom Either a deliberate fast zoom on air, or the way the director tells the camera operator to get the close-up as fast as possible.

Decibels (db) The units of sound measurement.

Detail See aperture correction.

Dichroic block A mix of glass layers that lets some colours through, and reflects others. Used in the front of cameras to split light into its separate primary colours.

Digital Signals that work in just '1s' and '0s'. Analogue signals can be converted to digital and vice versa.

Digital video effects (DVE) Machine used to whizz pictures around the screen.

Dissolve Old-fashioned term for a mix.

E to E Electronics to electronics. A way of seeing on the output of a video machine what is going into it without having to be recording.

EFP Electronic field production. Single camera with either separate or integral video recorder. While this may sound very similar to ENG it has a big difference. The word 'news' does not appear in the title, which makes some camera operators feel a lot better.

ENG Electronic news gathering. Single camera with either separate or integral video recorder. First used by news organisations to replace film cameras.

Extender An extra lens that can be switched in to extend the focal length of a lens.

Eyeline The direction in which a performer is looking in relation to the camera (i.e. their eyeline can be to the left/right, above/below the camera).

Field One half of a frame.

Fill One of the three main lights used, it softens the strong shadows from key lights and controls the contrast range.

Filter wheel A wheel holding a number of filters sitting just in front of the CCD. Typically it would hold neutral density and diffusion filters.

Focal length The distance behind a lens where parallel light rays converge.

Foldback The audio feed to the studio floor speakers.

Frame Two fields. There are 25 frames per second in a PAL signal, 30 for NTSC.

Gain Amplification that can be applied to either a video or an audio signal. It usually increases 'noise', making a video signal more grainy.

Gallery A production control room.

GV General view. Wide or long shots showing locations/local geography.

Hue The basic colour (i.e. red, yellow, orange etc.).

IFB Interrupt foldback. This is a sound feed (e.g. a programme clean feed going to a presenter at an OB) which someone (e.g. a director) can press a button and override. It is a nice easy way of being able to speak to the presenter through a single earpiece feed.

Kelvin (K) The unit of measurement used to describe colour temperature.

Key The main light for illumination and creating shadows.

LTC Longitudinal time code. The time code recorded horizontally along a VT.

Luminance The brightness of a television signal.

Lux The unit of measurement used to describe the amount of light received at a particular point.

M/E Mix effects. The part of the vision mixer where wipes and special effects are prepared.

Mixed minus (also known as Programme clean feed) The audio of programme output without one of the outside broadcast sources.

Monochrome Black and white television (or more accurately one colour, i.e. could be black and blue).

Neutral density filter A filter placed in front of a lens without altering the colour of the picture. It is used if you want to control the depth of field, or if you have an outrageously bright source.

Noise Electronic distortion added to either video or audio signals.

NTSC National Television System Committee. The people who defined the American television system.

Overscanning A television set which cuts off the edges of the picture. The opposite of underscanning, which shows the picture right the way into the corners. Underscanning is useful for checking that booms are not getting into shot.

PAL Television system used by much of Europe, India, Australia and many other countries.

PCF Programme clean feed. The studio output minus the live inject used by a presenter on location. The presenter can hear the whole programme without getting their own voice with a delay back in their ear.

Pedestal The base under a studio camera, commonly called a 'ped'.

PFL Pre-fade listen. A way of listening to an audio signal before it goes on air. Used by sound to check that a source is present. Directors sometimes use it to check the start of VT packages. Presenter listens are PFLs.

Pick-up Additional shots may be recorded at the end of a studio sequence. It is not always necessary to start from the beginning again, as long as there is a clean shot the editor can use to join the two recordings.

POV Point of view. A camera shot that mimics what one of the performers is seeing.

PSC Production single camera. Single camera with either separate or integral video recorder. I know that sounds just like ENG and EFP. It is.

Rx Record.

Saturation The amount of white mixed into the coloured light – 100% means it has no white light added.

SIS (Sound in syncs) A way of coding the sound into a video signal. Useful for outside broadcasts as it means that if the studio receives vision it will also definitely get the audio.

Soft light A light that gives faint or no shadows.

SOT Sound on tape.

SOVT Sound on video tape.

Standards converter The machine used to convert pictures from one TV system (PAL, NTSC or SECAM) into another.

Super Superimpose. Key a source over a background video.

Synchronous A vision source that can be used on air because it starts each field at the same time as all the other sources.

Tally light Vision mixers can send simple signals (tallies) to equipment e.g. cameras telling them when they have been cut on-air. The camera-mounted little red lights that use this signal are tally lights.

TBU Telephone balance unit. The device connected to telephone lines that enable presenters to have a phone conversation live on air.

Tight in/out The VT does not have a proper clean entry or exit point, i.e. instead of good clean silence and a steady shot at the beginning and end the editor may have had to put a freeze on, or didn't have time to clean up the sound.

Time-code Each frame of a VT is given a number in hours, minutes, seconds and frames. It provides a technique for finding shots and can be used by edit controllers.

TX Transmission/on air.

VITC (pronounced 'Vitsey') Vertical interval time-code. Time-code recorded in spare television lines, and used by edit controllers when they are jogging or slowing down tapes. VITC should read the same as LTC.

V/O Voice over.

White balance Electronic correction for lighting colour temperature, so a white object appears as white.

Lightning Source UK Ltd.
Milton Keynes UK
UKOW050617041011

179731UK00001B/34/A

9 780240 515250